ROUSSEAU

Confessions

PETER FRANCE

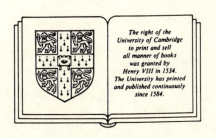

The right of the
University of Cambridge
to print and sell
all manner of books
was granted by
Henry VIII in 1534.
The University has printed
and published continuously
since 1584.

CAMBRIDGE UNIVERSITY PRESS

Cambridge
London   New York   New Rochelle
Melbourne   Sydney

Published by the Press Syndicate of the University of Cambridge
The Pitt Building, Trumpington Street, Cambridge CB2 1RP
32 East 57th Street, New York, NY 10022, USA
10 Stamford Road, Oakleigh, Melbourne 3166, Australia

First published 1987

Printed in Great Britain at
the University Press, Cambridge

British Library cataloguing in publication data

France, Peter. *1935–*
Rousseau: Confessions. – (Landmarks of world literature)
1. Rousseau, Jean-Jacques
I. Title II. Series
848′.508 PQ2043

Library of Congress cataloguing in publication data

France, Peter, 1935–
Rousseau, Confessions.
(Landmarks of world literature)
Bibliography.
1. Rousseau, Jean-Jacques, 1712–1778. Confessions.
2. Rousseau, Jean-Jacques, 1712–1778 – Biography.
3. Authors, French – 18th century – Biography.
4. Philosophers – France – Biography. 5. Autobiography.
I. Title. II. Series.
PQ2036.F7 1987 848′.509 86–11769

ISBN 0 521 32803 9 hard covers
ISBN 0 521 31500 X paperback

GG

Contents

Preface

'This frank and bold expression of the purest of souls . . .',
'This unparalleled monument of vanity and folly.' Such were
two contemporary reactions to the *Confessions*. Rousseau's
autobiography is certainly one of the landmarks of modern
literature; from the beginning, like its author, it has had the
power to divide people, to provoke love or hate, admiration
or contempt. This faces the reader with problems different
from those normally encountered in reading literary works. I
shall discuss these in chapter 5, but before withdrawing to
this distance, I shall try to enter Rousseau's world, outlining
the context, composition and aims of the *Confessions* in
chapters 1 and 2, and analysing the work from the double
point of view of form and meaning in chapters 3 and 4.

In what follows, I assume that readers are already
reasonably familiar with the *Confessions*. Quotations from
the text are given in my own translation; in the section dealing
with Rousseau's use of language I also quote longer passages
in French, and would urge any reader who knows French to
read the original, since Rousseau is one of the masters of the
language. Page references are to the standard French editions, the four volumes of the Bibliothèque de la Pléiade
Œuvres complètes under the general editorship of Marcel
Raymond and Bernard Gagnebin (quoted thus: I, 235) and
the complete correspondence, edited by Ralph Leigh and
published by the Voltaire Foundation (quoted thus: *Corr*.
XXX, 35).

It will be obvious how much I am indebted to a number of
scholars and critics; my thanks go also to those friends with
whom I have discussed questions raised in the following
pages, and particularly to John Renwick and Sian Reynolds,
who have read drafts of this book and helped me with their
comments.

PETER FRANCE

Chronology

Rousseau's life and publications		Major literary events		Important historical events	
28 June 1712	Jean-Jacques Rousseau born in Geneva. Mother dies a few days later.			1715	Death of Louis XIV, succeeded by Louis XV.
		1715–35	Alain René Lesage, Gil Blas.		
		1719	Daniel Defoe, Robinson Crusoe.		
		1721	Montesquieu, Persian Letters.		
1722	Father goes into exile.				
1722–4	At school in Bossey.				
1725–8	Apprenticeship in Geneva.	1726	Jonathan Swift, Gulliver's Travels.	1726–43	Cardinal Fleury Chief Minister of France.
1728	Leaves Geneva. First meeting with Madame de Warens. Becomes a Catholic convert in Turin.				
1728–31	Wandering, and a variety of jobs in Italy, Switzerland and France.	1731	Antoine Francois Prévost, Cleveland		
1731–40	Lives mainly in or near Chambéry, protected by Madame de Warens who becomes his mistress in 1733.	1731–41	Pierre Carlet de Chamblain de Marivaux, Life of Marianne		

	1733 Alexander Pope, *Essay on Man*	
	1734 Voltaire, *Philosophical Letters*	1735 Political disturbances in Geneva.
1737 Visit to Montepellier.	1739–40 David Hume, *Treatise of Human Nature*	1740–86 Reign of Frederick II of Prussia.
1740–1 Tutor in Lyon.		1740–8 War of Austrian Succession.
1742 Settles in Paris. Unsuccessful presentation of a new system of musical notation to the Academy of Science.		
1744–51 Makes a living as secretary, tutor and musician, protected by the Dupin family. Collaborates on the *Encyclopedia* and frequents Diderot, Condillac and other men of letters.		
1745 Beginning of liaison with Thérèse Levasseur.	1746 Etienne Bonnot de Condillac, *Essay on Human Knowledge.*	1745 Jacobite rising in Scotland.
	1748 Montesquieu, *Spirit of the Laws.*	
1749 'Vision' on the road to Vincennes.	1749 Samuel Richardson, *Clarissa Harlowe.*	

1751	Publication of the *Discourse on the Sciences and the Arts*. Beginning of his 'reform'.	1749	Henry Fielding, *Tom Jones*.
		1749	Denis Diderot, *Letter on the Blind*.
1752	Successful performance of *The Village Soothsayer* at Fontainebleau.	1749–88	George Louis Leclerc, Comte de Buffon, *Natural History*.
1754	Visits Geneva, returns to the Protestant church.	1751–72	*Encyclopedia*.
1755	Publication of the *Discourse on Inequality*.		1755 Lisbon earthquake.
1756	Moves to the Hermitage, invited by Madame d'Epinay.		1756–63 Seven Years War.
1757	Love for Madame d'Houdetot. Rousseau quarrels with Madame d'Epinay and Grimm, and leaves the Hermitage.		
1757–62	Living at Montlouis, near Montmorency, working on a series of major books.		1758–70 Duc de Choiseul effective First Minister of France.
1758	Publication of the *Letter to d'Alembert*. Break with Diderot.		

1759	Beginning of acquaintance with Luxembourgs.	1759 Voltaire, *Candide*.
1761	Publication of *La Nouvelle Héloïse*.	
1762	Publication of *Emile* and *The Social Contract*. Leaves France to avoid arrest.	1762 James Macpherson (Ossian), *Fingal*.
1762–5	Living in the region of Neuchâtel. Acquaintance with Earl Marischal Keith.	
1763	Publication of *Letter to the Archbishop of Paris*. Renounces Genevan citizenship.	
1764	Publication of *Letters from the Mountain*. Beginning of composition of the *Confessions*.	1764 Voltaire, *Philosophical Dictionary*.
1765	Driven from his house in Môtiers, takes refuge on the Island of Saint-Pierre.	
1766	Takes refuge in England. Quarrel with Hume.	1766 Oliver Goldsmith, *Vicar of Wakefield*.
1767	Takes refuge at Trye.	
1768–70	Living in the Dauphiné.	1768 Laurence Sterne, *Sentimental Journey*.
1770	Returns to Paris. Public readings of the *Confessions*.	

Historical events:

1762	'Civil war' in Geneva begins.
1762–96	Reign of Catherine II of Russia.
1764	Jesuit order dissolved in France.
1768	French annexation of Corsica.

1771			Maupeou reform of Paris *parlement*.
1772–6	Composition of the *Dialogues*.		
1774		Johann Wolfgang von Goethe, *Sorrows of Young Werther*.	Death of Louis XV, succeeded by Louis XVI.
1776		Adam Smith, *Wealth of Nations*.	American Declaration of Independence.
1776		Edward Gibbon, *Decline and Fall of the Roman Empire*.	
1776–8	Composition of *Reveries of the Solitary Walker*.		
2 July 1778	Dies at Ermenonville.		
1781		Immanuel Kant, *Critique of Pure Reason*.	
1781	Publication of Part I of the *Confessions* with the *Reveries*.		
1782		Choderlos de Laclos, *Dangerous Acquaintances*.	
1786		Robert Burns, *Poems*.	
1787		Bernardin de Saint-Pierre, *Paul and Virginia*.	
1789	Publication of Part II of the *Confessions*.		Fall of the Bastille.
1794	Rousseau's remains transferred to the Pantheon in Paris.		

Landmarks of world literature

Rousseau

CONFESSIONS

Landmarks of world literature

General Editor: J. P. Stern

Dickens: *Bleak House* – Graham Storey
Homer: *The Iliad* – Michael Silk
Dante: *The Divine Comedy* – Robin Kirkpatrick
Rousseau: *Confessions* – Peter France
Goethe: *Faust. Part One* – Nicholas Boyle
Woolf: *The Waves* – Eric Warner

FORTHCOMING
Cervantes: *Don Quixote* – Manuel Duran
Goethe: *The Sorrows of Young Werther* – Martin Swales
Constant: *Adolphe* – Dennis Wood
Balzac: *Old Goriot* – David Bellos
Mann: *Buddenbrooks* – Hugh Ridley
Pasternak: *Dr Zhivago* – Angela Livingstone
Marquez: *100 Years of Solitude* – Michael Wood

Chapter 1

Context: Rousseau's world and his books

In writing his *Confessions*, Rousseau wanted to 'say everything' about his life. It would therefore be pointless to begin a study of the book with a full biographical survey. The reader quickly comes to realise, however, that the work is not self-sufficient, and that the author takes for granted knowledge, whether of contemporary society or of his own writings, which not all modern readers possess. Moreover, his account stops in 1765, at the time when he was working on Part I of his autobiography and thirteen years before his death. The present chapter is meant therefore (together with the chronology on pp. vii–xi to provide a basic context for a reading of Rousseau's own story of his life.

Rousseau's world

An essential starting point is to remember that he was not a Frenchman, but a Genevan. Geneva was very different from Paris in the eighteenth century, and this difference is given emblematic status in his writing. His native city was a republic, albeit a tiny one, hemmed in by large monarchies and subject to continual pressure from France. The citizens were conscious of their democratic rights and duties, not the least of which was the defence of the fatherland. However, eighteenth-century Geneva was also the scene of violent internal conflicts between the dominant oligarchy, the Little Council, and the rest of the *citoyens et bourgeois*, the General Council, who saw their part in the government being taken over by a few leading families. After 1762, Rousseau came to play his part in this 'civil war', as one sees in Book 12 of the *Confessions*. Born into a family of watchmakers, he belonged to the middle rank of the bourgeoisie, by no means poor, but not one of the elite, and he always allied himself with the ordinary citizens of the General Council against the Little Council.

For Rousseau was by birth a *citizen* of Geneva, and he came to be known as *the* citizen of Geneva. He was proud to declare this title on the first page of most of his major writings until 1763. In that year, after two of his most important works had been condemned by the authorities of his homeland, he renounced his citizenship, but this was not to prevent him from painting Geneva as a lost paradise in the *Confessions*. Book 1 ends with an image of the life he might have led if he had never left home: 'I should have been a good Christian, a good citizen, a good father of a family, a good friend, a good worker, a good man in every way . . .' (I, 43).

'A good Christian': as well as being a republic, Geneva was the city of Calvin. The ministers exerted great authority, and the moral severity of their religion marked the everyday life of the people. This must have contributed to the readiness with which Rousseau experienced feelings of guilt – and tried to evade them. His own religious beliefs changed over the years. He became a Catholic convert after leaving Geneva, but returned to the Protestant fold when formally reassuming his citizenship in 1754. The personal creed he expounded a few years later in his 'Profession of Faith of a Savoyard Curate' (part of his *Emile*) is one of natural religion or deism, a rationally based faith in an all-powerful, intelligent and benevolent creator, and one which has no place for revelation; not surprisingly, it was condemned as unorthodox by the ministers of Geneva as well as by the Catholic church. Nevertheless, he continued to call himself a Christian, and his idiosyncratic faith supported him in the trials of his later years.

The deism of *Emile* is characteristic of the modernising movement in European thought that we now call the Enlightenment. Geneva was far from immune from such tendencies, as Rousseau recognised to his regret. But he himself, in his natural religion and in many other aspects of his thinking, was a participant in the Enlightenment he deplored. This is one of the many paradoxes which permeate his life and writing, and which he seeks to explain and justify in the *Confessions*. Another, related one is that the citizen of Geneva left Geneva in his sixteenth year and lived most of his life in the Catholic monarchies of Savoy and France. In particular he lived in the heart of the city that was for him the anti-Geneva, Paris, from 1742 to 1756 and from 1770 to 1778.

The span of Rousseau's life (1712–78), was almost the same as the reign of Louis XV (1715–74). In stark contrast to Geneva, Louis XV's France was an absolute monarchy. In some ways this arbitrary rule was perhaps less oppressive than that exercised by the authorities and public opinion in a small democracy, and Rousseau certainly found a kind of security in Paris at the end of his life, even though he was still officially liable to arrest under the 1762 sentence of the Paris *Parlement*, which had condemned his major work, *Emile*, and driven him into exile. This sentence, like the imprisonment of his friend Diderot for publishing subversive books, is a reminder that eighteenth-century France was not a tolerant country. Protestantism was outlawed there for most of the century.

At the period when Rousseau lived there, France was experiencing a period of prosperity and economic growth after the hardships which had marked Louis XIV's glorious reign. It was also a society of great inequalities of power, wealth and culture. Unlike many writers of the time, Rousseau the outsider knew at first hand many different sectors of this society, from peasant to prince. With characteristic exaggeration, he wrote that this gave his autobiography a particular value:

If we attach some importance to experience and observation, then I can claim to be in perhaps the most advantageous position any mortal has ever occupied, because having no specific station in life, I have known them all and lived in them all, from the lowest to the highest, except the throne.   (I, 1150)

Books 10 and 11 show him in 1760–2, when he was beginning to think of writing his memoirs, sharing his time between his rustic neighbours at Montmorency and his extremely exalted protectors and friends, the Luxembourgs and the Prince de Conti. Earlier he had been befriended by the aristocracy of wealth, the families of tax-farmers who were among the most generous patrons of the arts (at the expense of the poor tax-paying majority whom we glimpse in Book 4).

For Rousseau came to Paris at a time of great cultural and intellectual activity, and he quickly got to know some of those whose names now dominate the literary history of his age. At first he admired Voltaire, some thirty years his senior, and regarded in the 1740s as the successor of France's great tragic dramatists as well as a leading free-thinker, author of the *Philosophical Letters* (1734). Over the next thirty years, Voltaire was to become an increasingly vehement critic of political and legal abuses and of the Catholic church. His deism was not unlike Rousseau's, but the two men came to detest one another, and Voltaire subjected Rousseau to relentless abuse as a traitor to the cause of Enlightenment.

Among the *philosophes* (as the partisans of Enlightenment were known), the other dominant figure at this time was Montesquieu, author of the *Spirit of the Laws* (1748), a vast pioneer work in social science which is also a critique of despotism by a fervent admirer of the English constitution. England was indeed a source of inspiration to the *philosophes*; the work of Newton and Locke provided models which were developed by such writers as the mathematician Jean Le Rond d'Alembert (1717–83) and the philosopher Etienne Bonnot de Condillac (1715–80). There was also a powerful native tradition of critical thinking, in which the outstanding names are those of the sceptical Michel de Montaigne, whose *Essays* (1580–8) were one of the main influences on the *Confessions*, René Descartes, author of the radical *Discourse on Method* (1637), and Archbishop Fénelon, whose best-selling novel *Telemachus* (1699) was always one of Rousseau's favourite books.

The 1740s saw the beginning of the great French *Encyclopedia*. This collective enterprise, directed by Denis Diderot (1713–84) and published in seventeen folio volumes between 1750 and 1765, may be regarded as the epitome of the French Enlightenment. It was the work of a 'society of men of letters' − including Rousseau, who wrote on political economy and music − and was meant to provide a conspectus of the latest state of knowledge, not only in academic subjects, but in the useful arts also. Diderot hoped that it would 'change the general way of thinking'; in other words, it expressed the progressive values of the age, foremost among which were a critical attitude to current orthodoxies in all fields (above all religion) and a new stress on activities conducive to earthly happiness. Having been a junior member of the team, Rousseau set himself openly against the values of the Enlightenment in the *Discourse on the Sciences and the Arts* which brought him fame. He subsequently broke with the *philosophes* and came to consider them his bitterest enemies.

Traditional Geneva and modern Paris are the two poles of Rousseau's career. In addition he saw a good deal of Europe, both in his carefree young wanderings in Switzerland, France and Italy, and in his later flight from refuge to refuge in Switzerland, England and France. For the period up to October 1765, the detailed story is told in the *Confessions*, and there is no need to repeat it here, since Rousseau's account, having been called in question throughout the nineteenth century, has been largely vindicated by modern scholarship. While obviously open to correction on points of detail and on the way the narrator places the emphasis and interprets his story (I shall return to these questions in chapter 5), his text gives a reliable enough basic outline of his actions and movements. It will therefore be sufficient now to complete the story up to the end of Rousseau's life and to describe his other writings, since almost all of these are closely related to the *Confessions*.

Rousseau's life 1765–78

One needs to have some idea of Rousseau's life after 1765, since this was the period during which Part II of the *Confessions* was written and Part I was given its final form (the next chapter gives more details on the composition of the work). As the autobiography ends, the hero is just about to embark for England under the guidance of the Scottish philosopher David Hume (1711–76), a close friend of many of the Paris *philosophes*. This was to be a disastrous venture. All went well for a while, but Rousseau's demands for friendship were exorbitant and Hume was altogether a cooler character. Before long, the Genevan began to suspect his friend of being involved in a plot to discredit him. Living in relative isolation at Wootton in Derbyshire and understanding little English, Rousseau became obsessed with this idea, and on 10 July 1766 he sent an immense and dramatic letter accusing Hume of treachery. The tone of it can be seen from the following extract:

Although I am to be pitied, I am less so than you, and my only vengeance is to leave you with the torment of respecting in spite of yourself the poor man on whom you have heaped misfortune.

(*Corr*. XXX, 46)

Naturally outraged, Hume seems to have over-reacted, and thanks partly to the malice of some of his Parisian friends, the quarrel soon became the talk of Europe. The Scot published his own *Concise Account* of the affair, but Rousseau refused to defend himself publicly, deliberately isolating himself at Wootton, where he spent his time botanising and writing the *Confessions*.

Then in the spring of 1767, in an access of panic, he fled from England and took refuge under a false name in the château of the Marquis de Mirabeau at Trye on the edge of Normandy. His stay there became as nightmarish as his months in England. Persuaded that he was the victim of a universal conspiracy, he went to the Grenoble region in 1768 and spent two winters in the vicinity of the small town of Bourgoin. Here in 1768 he unofficially 'married' Thérèse Levasseur, his companion for the previous twenty-three years, and in the winter of 1769–70 wrote Part II of the *Confessions*. The following summer, defying prudent counsels, he returned openly to Paris to give public readings of his autobiography. After a few sessions further readings were forbidden by the authorities, but otherwise he was not much molested and lived quietly with Thérèse in a small apartment until the year of his death.

For about the last twelve years of his life, Rousseau believed himself to be the object of a conspiracy to blacken his name and distort his message. I shall discuss his vision of the plot in chapter 4, but it is worth emphasising at the outset that it was a fantasy. He was indeed the object of repressive measures and malicious misrepresentation, but all this falls a long way short of a conspiracy of which every man, woman or child who approached him was believed to be an instrument. In so far as such labels help, it seems fair to describe him in his later years as the victim of a persecution mania. This does not mean that his whole mental world was blacked out by madness. His delusion provided him with an objection-proof system for interpreting other people's actions, but it did not affect all his perceptions and attitudes. His correspondence at this time and the descriptions of his behaviour by visitors and friends often show a Rousseau very different from the haunted author of the opening lines of Book 12 of the *Confessions*. Indeed Hume concluded from accounts of his calm and cheerful behaviour at Wootton, at the very time when he was accusing his friend of the blackest treason, that he was simply acting out a part. At the very least we have to assume, as a reading of the *Confessions* confirms, that his was a complex, contradictory nature.

Something similar might be said about Rousseau's illnesses. 'I was born nearly dying . . .': one could get the impression from his autobiography that his whole life was dogged by ill health. Now these ailments were real ones, whether or not their origin was psychosomatic. His bladder complaint (retention of urine) caused him great pain, inconvenience and worry, so much so that he periodically thought himself at death's door. But it seems certain not only that he was quick to imagine future suffering, but also that he tended to exaggerate his illnesses, his insomnia for instance. Hume remarks (in a letter written before the quarrel) that although he thinks himself 'very infirm', Rousseau is 'one of the

most robust men I have ever known' (*Corr*. XXVIII, 203).
He could spend months (usually in winter) confined to his
room, but remained a vigorous walker until the end of his
life.

Rousseau's other writings

It may be possible to regard the *Confessions* as the lay
equivalent of a hagiography with the writer as saint, but it is
hardly an author's autobiography in the sense of 'an account
of how I wrote my books'. The composition and contents of
Rousseau's writing take up a fairly small part of the total text.
The author assumes that the readers will know his works, and
that this is one of their reasons for wanting to know about his
life (his second autobiographical book, the *Dialogues*, ex-
plicitly sets out to relate the life to the works). The reader
therefore needs some acquaintance, preferably at first hand,
with the more important of his earlier books. The following
pages are meant simply as a brief guide.

Rousseau's first writings, which are of no great interest in
themselves, date back to the time at Chambéry when he gave
himself the literary and philosophical education he had
missed in childhood. He was different from most men of
letters of his day in being largely self-taught; not having been
through the usual scholastic mill, he says he found
composition difficult, but this disadvantage was outweighed
by the fact that he read widely and eclectically out of desire
rather than duty, and that his natural eloquence was not
subjected too early to the disciplines of good taste and
correctness. It also meant that he was a late beginner. To his
contemporaries in Paris in the 1740s he was 'Rousseau the
musician'. Music was indeed one of the great loves of his life;
not only did it bring him fame with the success of his opera
The Village Soothsayer, it also provided him with a
consolation and indeed a livelihood (as a copyist) for much
of his life. By contrast he liked to present book-writing as a
vocation thrust upon him by his 'illumination' on the road to

Vincennes in 1749, a sudden disturbing irruption into a peaceful life.

The great period of what he calls his 'doctrinal' works is quite short, extending from 1749 to the condemnation of *Emile* in 1762. It begins with the prize-winning *Discourse on the Sciences and the Arts*, published in 1750. In this academic piece, the first expression of his new vision, Rousseau argues that intellectual, artistic and technological progress has not improved the moral condition of humanity, indeed that the various 'arts' (from eloquence to goldsmithing) have their origins in human vices and tend to corrupt morals. His thought is not fully worked out here; the success of the discourse was due to its provocative thesis and somewhat swollen eloquence rather than to any great argumentative force. In the subsequent polemic, however, he went to the root of the problem as he saw it. The result was his second academic discourse, the *Discourse on the Origins of Inequality among Men*. This is one of his fundamental works, and it throws a great deal of light on his presentation of his own life.

The starting point can perhaps be seen in the final words of the *Discourse*: 'it is manifestly against the Law of Nature, however we define it, that a child should command an old man, that an imbecile should direct a wise man, and that a handful of people should wallow in unnecessary luxuries while the starving multitude lacks the basic necessities of life' (III, 194). Such is Rousseau's vision of modern society. It seems to him evident that there is no justifiable connection between the scandalous inequalities of society as we know it and the natural (physical or mental) inequality between one person and another. His aim, therefore, in attempting to explain the origins of inequality will be 'to mark in the progress of things the moment when Right took the place of Violence, and Nature was submitted to Law; to explain by what series of prodigies the strong man could bring himself to serve the weak and the people to purchase an imaginary peace at the cost of their real happiness' (III, 132).

A hypothetical history of humanity offers a key to

understanding our present discontents. Rousseau constructs a model of 'natural man', and this means stripping off the accretions of time and society which have encrusted our original nature like the submerged statue of the sea-god Glaucus, 'which time, the sea and storms had so disfigured that it looked less like a God than a ferocious beast' (III, 122). The parallel with Rousseau's search for his true self in the *Confessions* will be obvious. But how does the author of the *Discourse* propose to gain access to man's lost nature? Partly by deductions from recent anthropological accounts of newly discovered peoples, but principally by *introspection*. His workplace was the Forest of Saint Germain: 'Deep in the forest I sought and found the image of the earliest times' (I, 388). What he found was the image of a humanity that is *naturally good*.

The idea of natural goodness is central in Rousseau's writing. As against the Christian doctrine of original sin or the notion of natural aggression put forward by the English philosopher Thomas Hobbes, he presents the following postulate:

Meditating on the first and simplest operations of the human soul, I believe I can see in them two principles which precede the use of reason: the first attaches us passionately to our well-being and preservation, the second inspires in us a natural disinclination to see any sentient being, and principally our fellow human beings, perish or suffer.   (III, 125)

Living in a pre-social state, as yet incapable of speech or thought, guided by these two instincts, 'love of self' and pity, human beings are *good*, because they have no desire to harm one another. They are not *virtuous*, because virtue implies the willed overcoming of passion in the interest of others, and this comes only with the development of society and reason. While subject to natural forces such as disease or climate, they are independent of one another's will, since domination and servitude can only come into existence with social organisation.

The first half of the *Discourse* is devoted to elaborating this picture of natural humanity. The second is a more truly historical — and increasingly nightmarish — account of the evolution of society, the development of the family, tribal living, agriculture and metallurgy, the division of labour, property, law, and all the subsequent oppressions of the poor by the rich. As for the moral development of men and women, the crucial shift is from the original 'love of self' (*amour de soi*) to sophisticated 'self-love' (*amour-propre*). By the latter term is meant the tendency of people in society to compare themselves with others, and to seek their happiness in the admiration and envy of others and in the power they can exert over them. This is the source of the aggressive passions, hate, envy, jealousy, cruelty. For Rousseau these are not natural passions, but distortions inflicted on our original instincts by the pressures of society — and above all by bad social organisation.

The mood of the *Discourse* is dark; one of Rousseau's basic contentions is that there is no way of reversing the historical process, no way of going 'back to Nature' (a slogan often wrongly associated with his name). As for going forward, the *Discourse* offers little hope. It is worth noting however that in his sketch of human history, Rousseau does single out an early 'savage' stage of tribal life, a 'happy mean' which he calls the 'true youth of the world' and the 'age of gold' (III, 171). This suggests that it may after all be possible to live happily in society; this promise is echoed, in a different way, by the dedication of the work to an idealised political society, the Republic of Geneva. Rousseau's subsequent writings continue in this more positive vein. After the denunciations of the two discourses comes a series of efforts to envisage ways either of limiting the damage done by society or of constructing a new social life which will replace our lost happiness by equivalent or greater benefits. The most important of these are the *Letter to d'Alembert*, the *Social Contract, Emile* and *Julie (La Nouvelle Héloïse)*.

The first of these to be completed was the *Letter*, a refutation of d'Alembert's suggestion in the *Encyclopedia* that Genevan society would be improved by the establishment of a theatre. Rousseau's specific arguments about the theatre expand into more general considerations about the good society. Writing just after his break with the *philosophes*, he takes the opportunity to criticise the Parisian world of false appearances and corruption and to reassert the traditional values he associates with Switzerland – simplicity, useful work, affection, family life, piety. Seen from the point of view of the *Discourse on Inequality*, Geneva represents an earlier, happier stage in the development of humanity towards 'the apparent perfection of the individual' and 'the real decrepitude of the species' (III, 171). In writing the *Letter*, Rousseau is simply trying to stop or slow down this apparently inexorable process of degeneration. As he does so, he continues the identification of himself with Geneva which was begun in the dedication to the earlier work, and in both texts an idealised image of the author's father serves as a link between himself and his lost community.

A Genevan element is present too, though less openly, in another of the major works of this period, the *Social Contract*. In this discussion of political theory, Rousseau claimed to have been thinking of his native city, not so much in its reality of 1760 as in its original constitutional form. In other respects, the *Social Contract*, one of the most abstract of his writings, is the work least obviously linked with the *Confessions*. It concerns the 'principles of political right' and in particular the problem formulated as follows:

To find a form of association which will defend and protect with the force of the whole community the person and goods of each associate, and through which each one in uniting with all will nevertheless obey only himself and remain as free as before. (III, 360)

The solution is found in the rule of law, based on the general will of the citizens. This is not a blueprint for action, though it provided a point of reference for its author's subsequent constitutional writings on Corsica and Poland; it constructs instead a theoretical model, just as the *Discourse on Inequality* proposes a model of natural humanity. For Rousseau, this political model had been most nearly approached in the republics of antiquity, Sparta and Rome – and perhaps modern Geneva. Seen in relation to modern France, England or Savoy, it could only be a yardstick by which their political arrangements were found wanting. And for the author of the *Confessions* it was no longer a practical option. If he had a personal goal in the 1760s, it was closer to the independence of the state of nature than to the law-governed freedom of the *Social Contract*.

His two most substantial books of this period are both much more closely connected with the *Confessions*. The first, *Emile*, is subtitled 'On Education', but it is far more than a pedagogical treatise. Rousseau himself called it a 'treatise on the original goodness of man' (III, 934). As this implies, it embodies the same view of natural goodness and social corruption as the *Discourse on Inequality*. But now Rousseau goes beyond the negative vision of the earlier work and looks for possible ways forward, not in an impossible ideal state, but in the real world of France. What can be done to keep the child and adolescent as near as possible to 'nature'? Is it feasible to check the growth of self-love in society? And can one hope to reconcile the supposed solitary independence of nature with the virtuous affections which are so crucial to social happiness? To suggest answers to these questions, Rousseau again constructs a model, not an abstract model now, but the figure of a boy set in a world full of individuals and objects. The treatise develops into a novel.

Emile and the *Confessions* should be read together; in conjunction they provide a rich meditation on the questions of childhood and education. They have in common Rousseau's radical readiness to give weight to childhood for its own sake, rather than as a training period for future adults. He writes in *Emile*: 'Humanity has its place in the order of things; childhood has its place in the order of human life; we should consider the man in the man and the child in the child' (IV, 303). It is not surprising, therefore, that the *Confessions* is one of the first biographical narratives, whether historical or fictional, to attach real importance to a period of life which most people today recognise as crucial, but whose significance was only recognised by a few pioneering spirits in the eighteenth century.

If one compares the two works, one realises that the 'treatise' is partly a compensation for what was missing in the author's own life. Emile has the healthy upbringing and the continuing protective care that Jean-Jacques enjoyed only spasmodically, while his tutor is the successful educator and powerful father-figure that Rousseau never became. But the author of Emile draws on his own life experience in a direct way too. He refers to an episode from his stay at Bossey, to his attempts to be a teacher and to his knowledge of peasant children; in addition the lengthy 'Profession of Faith of a Savoyard Curate' relates directly to his own searchings and to his meetings with the Abbés Gaime and Gatier (recorded in Book 3 of the *Confessions*). But the most fascinating overlap comes in the unfinished sequel to *Emile*, a fictional work of 1762 entitled *The Solitaries* or *Emile and Sophie*. Here the hero of *Emile*, having been happily married at the end of the previous book, is seen plunged in a state of solitary despair by his wife's infidelity. He draws on his education to lead a life of stoical independence, free of illusory hope, and in doing so, he speaks with the same words and in the same tone that Rousseau will use some years later in his autobiographical writings.

The long and immensely successful novel, *La Nouvelle Héloïse*, anticipates the autobiography in similar ways. Book 9 of the *Confessions* describes the writing of the novel in some detail, showing how it came out of lived experience as well as dreams − and how it prefigured or even sparked off the author's real-life love for Madame d'Houdetot. Saint-Preux, the hero of *La Nouvelle Héloïse*, is clearly Rousseau. He is made younger, nobler, more dashing, but he still embodies some of the weaknesses described in the *Confessions*. And just as Emile is brought to a state of balanced happiness that his creator could never achieve, so Saint-Preux in the second part of the novel is steered out of the stormy waters of destructive passion into the calm haven of a virtuous *ménage à trois* after Rousseau's own heart. The ideal world of Clarens is a projection to be set alongside the half-remembered, half-imagined paradise of Les Charmettes in Book 6 of the

Confessions. They are not identical, but the resonance between the two is striking. The same could be said of many themes, images, proper names (e.g. Claude Anet) or anecdotes (e.g. the visit to the Paris brothel) which link the two works. There was a time when Rousseau's autobiographical writing was seen as belonging to another world from that of the discourses, the treatises and even the novel: it has become increasingly obvious to modern commentators that the different works derive from a common, if complex, vision of things and are mutually illuminating.

After the publication of *Emile* in 1762, however, Rousseau's writing did change direction. Until then he had been working out the implications of the vision of things revealed to him on the road to Vincennes. He had written out of his own experience, to be sure, but generally through the mediation of discursive prose or fiction. From 1762 onwards, with the exception of relatively minor (though still important) works, such as his *Dictionary of Music* or his political writings on Corsica and Poland, his main efforts as an author went into scrutinising and describing his life and character, presenting himself directly to the public, justifying himself. Particularly interesting in this respect are two works which bridge the gap between the publishing of *Emile* and the beginning of serious work on the *Confessions*. Both take the form of letters and were written in self-defence. The *Letter to the Archbishop of Paris* (1763) is a brilliant polemic directed at Archbishop Beaumont's condemnation of *Emile*. And in the *Letters from the Mountain*, published in 1764, Rousseau turns his fire against his Genevan critics, defending the religious views expressed in *Emile* and the politics of the *Social Contract*. Both are contributions to public debate; they concern the books, not the man. But autobiography is never far away. The *Letter to the Archbishop* opens with reflections on 'the oddities of my destiny', includes a portrait of the author as good, weak, loving, free, devout and honest, and cites St Augustine's *Confessions* on the duty of truth-telling. In the *Letters from the Mountain*, as in the preamble to the *Confessions*, he imagines a last judgement at which he would appear holding his book, and defies 'the abominable man who dares to boast that he sees evil [in my heart], where it has never been'. Here also we find a brief indication of one of the main problems facing the autobiographer; Rousseau is convinced of the purity of his intentions in writing books branded as subversive, but he says ruefully: 'I cannot show the good that I feel in my heart' (III, 696). The time was ripe for him to take up all the autobiographical hints scattered through his earlier writings. He was to devote the second half of his writing career above all to writing about himself.

Chapter 2

Autobiography: the composition and aims of the '*Confessions*'

The three autobiographies

Most writers are content with one autobiography, the final summation of a life. Others repeat the exercise; perhaps they are dissatisfied with the first attempt, perhaps they acquire a taste for writing about themselves. Rousseau is one of the latter. The *Confessions*, his first full-length autobiographical writing, was followed by two others, both of them quite different in kind. The three works should ideally be read as a series; taken together they show a fascinating evolution in the enterprise of understanding the self and presenting it to the world. Before coming to the composition and aims of the *Confessions*, let me say a few words about its two sequels, the *Dialogues* and the *Reveries*.

The first of the three works had been completed in 1770. Rousseau gave public readings of it in Paris, but these did not achieve what he had hoped for. The last lines of the text as we have it give a saddening glimpse of the embarrassment and silence which greeted his attempt to communicate his vision of himself. In 1772 therefore he embarked on a second instalment, the strangest of all his books, known as the *Dialogues* or *Rousseau, Judge of Jean-Jacques*. This is not a first-person narrative, but a fictional conversation which resembles a court hearing. The two protagonists are 'Rousseau' and 'the Frenchman'; the subject of their conversation is 'Jean-Jacques', the strange and apparently monstrous author known to the public at large. 'Jean-Jacques' does not appear as a character in the dialogues, but there are quotations from his books and from speeches attributed to him. The point of this elaborate staging is to allow Rousseau to give a professedly objective account of himself, to imagine the most damning criticisms of his behaviour and to refute them, so that finally he can overcome the imaginary splitting of the self in a picture of his life and works as a unified and innocent whole. Dominated by the idea of the conspiracy which already figures prominently in Part II of the *Confessions*, this is a dark and tortuous book, painful to read because of its exaggeration and repetition, but containing moments of brilliant intensity and vision.

The final work, the *Reveries of the Solitary Walker*, is very different. It was written between 1776 and Rousseau's death in 1778. Having finished the *Dialogues*, he was anxious above all to deposit them in safe keeping, so that even if he could not reach the ears of his contemporaries, he would be able to speak to posterity. He decided therefore to place a hand-written copy on the altar at Notre Dame, but when he went to do this, he found his way barred by a metal screen he had not previously seen. He interpreted this as a sign from God that he was not to succeed in changing people's minds about him. He resigned himself to his fate, and the *Reveries* are the fruit of this resignation. Where the two earlier works had been directed towards a reader or a listener, in this last work Rousseau set out to write for himself. Even if self-justification surfaces frequently, in the ten meditations or 'walks' which make up the book, the dominant motifs are the search for the true self and the reconstitution in writing of the happiness of existence. The author is still the obsessed person of Part II of the *Confessions* and the *Dialogues*, but it is as if he has finally won through to the other side of the nightmare and reached an intermittently sunlit place where he can take pleasure in being himself − and in writing.

Composition of the *Confessions*

Although written over three or four years, the *Dialogues* are the product of a single impulse of self-justification; the *Reveries* are a multi-faceted self-portrait composed in a fairly short space of time. Unlike these two sequels, the *Confessions*, while possessing the unity of a linear narrative, have the complexity which comes of being written over a fairly long period, during which their author's situation and aims in writing changed considerably. It is helpful for the reader to have an idea of this complicated process, because the *Confessions*, like most autobiographies, refer constantly not only to the period written about, but also, if less overtly, to the period of writing.

Like certain modern novels, this autobiography does in fact recount its own beginnings. The subject is first introduced in Book 10, where Rousseau, writing about the year 1759 or 1760, notes:

For some strange reason Rey [his publisher] had been urging me for some time to write my memoirs. Although they were not up to that time particularly interesting in terms of events, I realised that they could become interesting through the frankness which I was capable of devoting to the task; and I decided to make of them a work unique in its unparalleled truthfulness.   (I, 516)

Rousseau's correspondence, together with the work of Madame Hermine de Saussure and other Rousseau scholars, allows one to trace the origins and composition of the book in more detail.

The previous chapter indicated that what one may call the autobiographical impulse is present in many of his earlier writings. There are indeed anticipations of the *Confessions* in minor works of the 1740s, but the move to autobiography begins in earnest somewhat later, around 1756. Book 9 tells how Rousseau's memories of earlier years were revived when he went to live at the Hermitage, and it is probably from this period that one can date the earliest of his surviving auto-biographical fragments. Soon afterwards, his quarrel with Madame d'Epinay, Grimm and the *philosophes* increased his need to open his heart and to defend his name. He began now to take more care of letters received or sent. This was to be an essential part of his autobiographical task; in 1762 he started to copy out all the letters he wished to keep into special manuscript books, which were designed not only to 'help me to remember facts and dates in the correct order' (I, 607), but to be published alongside his memoirs. Eventually he gave up this idea and stopped copying (see the end of Book 10), but he made extensive use of his papers in Part II of the *Confessions*.

Although he was thinking of writing his life as early as 1759 or 1760, Rousseau's energies in the years up to 1762 were taken up by his other books. In that year, however, he was virtually forced into writing about himself. Book 11 describes the tormenting circumstances in which he sent to the sympathetic government official Malesherbes four eloquent and fascinating letters, which are like a summary of the memoirs he thought he would not live to write. It was, however, only in 1764, when he had finished the *Letter to the Archbishop* and the *Letters from the Mountain*, that he really got down to writing the complete narrative account of his life. By the end of that year he had probably drafted a good deal of Part I. Then in December 1764 he received a copy of the *Sentiments of the Citizens*, described in Book 12 as 'an anonymous paper that seemed to have been written not with ink but with the water of Phlegeton' (I, 632). Phlegeton was a river in the pagan hell, and though Rousseau did not know it, this hellish pamphlet was the work of Voltaire. It accused him of madness, indecency, irreligion, megalomania, ingratitude, subversive behaviour, debauchery. Rousseau was outraged, but at the same time the fact that this work divulged secrets he had entrusted to his former friends (including Madame d'Epinay) removed his earlier scruples about harming others by his confessions. He was now free to speak openly and to defend himself.

In 1765, therefore, he began to write out a fair copy of Part I. We do not know for sure how he worked, but no doubt he had previously made drafts – in some cases several of these have survived for a single incident (for instance the scene with Madame Basile in Turin). He may then have worked these up into a continuous narrative in one or more manuscripts before making a fair copy. The essential point, however, is that the existing manuscripts of the *Confessions* were made some time after the text was first drafted – and for some sections many years later. As far as Part I is concerned,

Rousseau began a fair copy before leaving for England in December 1765 and continued it at Wootton, at the same time as his quarrel with Hume. This is known as the Neuchâtel manuscript, and differs considerably from the definitive version; in particular it contains a very interesting declaration of aims (written in 1764) which I shall refer to henceforward as the Neuchâtel preamble.

For some unknown reason, Rousseau abandoned this manuscript half-way through Book 4, but continued to work on Part I (Books 1–6), which was generally composed with much greater care than Part II (Books 7–12). Book 6 was written at the Chateau of Trye after he had fled panic-stricken from England to France; in writing it, he did not have his other manuscripts with him, which helps to explain certain inconsistencies and repetitions between Books 5 and 6. It is worth remembering that the *Confessions* were written and copied out, not in the security of a permanent home, but on the run, in a series of temporary resting places. Rousseau had constant trouble in getting hold of the documents he needed. What is more, he knew that his enemies were apprehensive about what he was writing, and he feared that they would cut off his life-line to the public by stealing his papers or tampering with the text of his memoirs.

By the end of 1767 he had apparently drafted all of Part I, a good deal of Book 7, and probably some passages from the later books. Then, whether out of despair or resignation, he abandoned the enterprise for a year or more. At the end of 1768, living now at Bourgoin in the Dauphiné, he seems to have begun a new fair copy of his work, and it was probably at this time that he replaced the Neuchâtel preamble by the definitive introduction, which bears all the marks of his state of paranoia. Between 1768 and 1770 his vision of the conspiracy grew and deepened. In November 1769, after a gap of two years, he began composing again. Most of Part II was written in a matter of three or four months, and the whole work was virtually complete by the time he left the Dauphiné in April 1770. It seems that he had overcome his fear or caution, and decided to cast aside his pseudonym and go

heroically to Paris to confront the 'enemy' with his confessions. He wrote rapidly now, in a state of anxiety which
surfaces in passages such as this:

The ceilings over me have eyes, the walls around me have ears; surrounded by malevolent and vigilant spies and watchdogs, anxious
and distracted, I hastily scribble down a few broken words which I
barely have time to reread, let alone correct.   (I, 279)

As these prefatory remarks to Book 7 show, Rousseau was
aware that the second part was a rushed job, less well written
than the first, over which its only advantage (as he saw it) was
the importance of the subject – the righting of injustice.

Not only did he compose most of Part II in these winter
months, he also wrote out the greater part of the two existing
fair copies of the complete work. These are known as the
Paris and Geneva manuscripts; they differ in details, the
Geneva copy being a little fuller, but both are executed with
meticulous care. One is struck by their smallness; the two
Paris volumes are hardly more than notebooks, in which
every inch of space is filled with rows of tiny but always legi-
ble handwriting. Both of these definitive versions differ considerably from the Neuchâtel manuscript of the first three-
and-a-half books, and for some passages, such as the spanking scene in Book 1, a comparison of the texts is very sug-
gestive. Once the final copies were made, Rousseau continued
for several years to add footnotes to them – often ironic
comments on his own earlier naivety.

The penultimate act of this long story is the public
readings. In his attempt to obtain justice, Rousseau gave at
least four of these, concentrating on Part II, which contained
the most controversial material and few of the obscene incidents that would have been unacceptable in a mixed social
gathering. There were various reactions to these sessions; the
one that left the deepest mark was that described on the last
page of the text: 'I finished my reading, and everyone remained silent. Madame d'Egmont was the only person who seemed
moved; she trembled visibly, but quickly recovered and said
nothing, like the rest of the company. Such was the only
result I achieved with this reading and my declaration'

(I, 656). He had to move on to the *Dialogues*. But for the *Confessions* the last act came after his death. He had insisted that they should be published posthumously, and had asked for publication of Part II to be delayed until the year 1800. In the event Part I came out with the *Reveries* in 1782 and Part II in 1789.

What does one learn from this complicated story? A certain critical orthodoxy would suggest that what matters to the reader is the text on the page, the finished work, however it came to be written. This seems to me a limited view. It is surely desirable also to see the *Confessions* as an *act* on Rousseau's part, one that lasted many years and went through several different phases. In this way one can understand better some of the contradictions and unevennesses of the printed text. For instance, in writing out his fair copies, Rousseau did not attempt to homogenise his work; he added remarks, but tended to leave intact references to earlier phases in the writing. Any given page may therefore bear the mark of several different moments: the moment being described, the time of first drafting, that of the fair copy and perhaps the moment when a footnote was added. The book contains a history of the author's life from 1712 to 1765, but also, indirectly, a history of the time of its composition, from 1756 to 1770 and beyond, as he fled from Montmorency to Môtiers, to the Island of Saint-Pierre, to England, to Trye, to the Dauphiné and back to Paris. His book is not a disinterested aesthetic creation (if such a thing exists). In part it can be understood as the working through of problems which came from his inheritance, childhood and early life, but it is in large part a reaction to events from 1756 to 1770, to quarrels, friendships, criticism, persecution, and to such publications as Voltaire's *Sentiments of the Citizens* or Hume's *Concise Account*. In response to all this the very conception of an autobiographical work was bound to vary.

Aims

Certainly there is no single aim underlying the entire work.

Readers who say that the whole thing is an elaborate attempt at self-aggrandisement, for instance, are reducing it, the better to dismiss it. Nor can one really say, as has been argued in the past, that the *Confessions* began with one aim (self-knowledge) and deviated into another (self-justification). One should rather think of Rousseau as moved more or less simultaneously by several different impulses. I shall distinguish four of these, all of which the author acknowledges. They can mainly be related to existing traditions in autobiography and to classic models, and can be labelled respectively: confession, self-justification, self-knowledge and pleasure.

The title of the work is immediately arresting. Not 'memoirs' or 'the story of my life', but 'confessions'. In fact Rousseau often uses the other two descriptions in letters and even in the text of the work, where the words 'confess' and 'confession' are fairly infrequent (particularly in Part I). The title is an unmistakeable reference to one of the great Christian writings, the *Confessions* of St Augustine (*c.* 397). The Saint's work is addressed to God for the edification of men. It is full of the Scriptures, which provide a framework for understanding the author's life, his sins, his struggles and above all his conversion. The narrative is beautifully organised to convey a meaning. It is a confession in two senses: a confession of sins and a confession (or profession) of faith; the two are inseparable, as it is God's treatment of the sinner that justifies the faith.

In the seventeenth and eighteenth centuries many confessional narratives were written, not necessarily for publication, particularly by unorthodox religious believers such as pietists, methodists or quietists – those for whom the inner life was of most importance. From his early years in Geneva and Savoy Rousseau may have known this tradition. But in spite of the title, his *Confessions* are not like those of the Saint and the pietists. They may perhaps be regarded as a secular version of a confession of faith, with the hero sinning and straying and discovering the truth, but almost certainly this meaning was not intended by the author. 'Confessions' in the plural refers to the confession of sins, and it is in this that Rousseau's practice diverges from Christian confession.

In the first place he does not confess to God. On the first page he does indeed paint a scene of judgement, at which he will appear before the 'sovereign judge', confessions in hand. But until that time he speaks to his fellow-men, his readers or listeners, and it is to them that he lays bare his actions and feelings. This is compatible of course with a Protestant tradition of public confession, and the final lines of the preamble imagine a scene of reciprocal confession – he will tell his sins, then everybody else will tell theirs. But to what end? To gain forgiveness, would be a normal Christian answer, and this may be in Rousseau's mind too, but he tends to speak rather of gaining relief. This is how he puts it at the end of Book 2, after recounting the incident of the ribbon: 'This weight has therefore remained unrelieved on my conscience to this day, and I can say that the desire to unburden myself of it has played a great part in my decision to write my confessions' (I, 86). The same is true of other shameful incidents in his past, his sexual adventures perhaps, but more particularly those where he acted meanly, disloyally or inhumanly. This may be the case with the abandoning of his children (in spite of his declared belief that this action was justified); certainly he had already felt the need to reveal this behaviour both to certain acquaintances and – with a stress on his remorse – in an indirect passage in the *Emile*. More generally, as he himself says, he was a person who needed to bare his breast and took pleasure in doing so. He remarks at one point: 'a continual need to confide is constantly bringing my heart to my lips' (I, 156) – the word he uses being *épanchement*, the spilling of one's secrets into the willing ear and heart of a benevolent listener. In the *Confessions* he shows himself at several points gaining relief from such outpourings, whether to 'Maman', to the French Ambassador at Soleure, or to Thérèse after his visit to a brothel.

What is more, in his eyes confession seems to wipe out the crime — as if by an inversion of the French proverb: 'Qui s'excuse, s'accuse.' Rousseau appears to believe (and he is not the only one) that when he has accused himself, no one else has the right to accuse him. It is a pre-emptive strike. He remarks in Book 12, referring to the declaration about his children in *Emile*: 'When I had written like this, it is surprising that anyone had the courage to reproach me with it [his fault]' (I, 594). The sinner confessing his sins ceases to be a contrite creature seeking God's forgiveness and becomes a heroic figure, braving public ignominy to tell the truth. The tactic does not always work however; having finished the ribbon episode with the words: 'Let me be allowed never to speak of it again' (I, 87), he still felt obliged to return to the same incident in the fourth 'Walk' of the *Reveries*. Confession cannot always cancel out guilt.

Immediately after the passage about the weight of guilt quoted earlier, we read the words:

I have not beaten about the bush in what I have said so far, and it will surely not be thought that I have tried to disguise the wickedness of my crime. But I would not be fulfilling the aim of this book if I did not at the same time reveal my inner feelings and if I was afraid to excuse myself in so far as this is compatible with the truth.

(I, 86)

The move from confession to self-justification is rapid, and the convoluted style here may betray some discomfort at this, but Rousseau does go on to mitigate his crime, suggesting that his motives were not malicious − and for him it was the intention, not the outcome, which determined the value of behaviour. He frequently defends himself in this way and in chapter 4 I shall outline some of the explanatory schemes he invokes. At times he goes further and ends up by presenting actions for which he has felt remorse as justifiable or even praiseworthy. Thus the writing of a novel is in contradiction with his principles, but *La Nouvelle Héloïse* is in fact an edifying work. And on the vexed question of his children (which seems to be the aspect of his confessions which has shocked most readers), he gives reasons for believing that in placing them in the Foundlings' Home he was really acting in their best interests. Then, realising perhaps that he has been protesting too much, he concludes this episode with the words:

'I have promised my confessions, not my justification; I will therefore say no more. My task is to be true, the reader's is to be just. That is all I shall ever ask of him' (I, 359).

Notice here how the reader is made a judge. The concern for being rightly judged (a common motive in autobiography) is central to Rousseau's writing about himself — above all in *Rousseau Judge of Jean-Jacques*, but also in the *Confessions*. This affects Part I as well as Part II, but it naturally concerns primarily those aspects of his later life which were already known to the public. In his view, these were generally misrepresented. As he wrote, he could read or hear about the hostile accounts of his character and behaviour which circulated all over Europe. It was natural for him therefore to take up the stance of counsel for the defence as he dealt with such episodes as his quarrel with Madame d'Epinay, Grimm and the *philosophes* (they were to do much the same, though rather less scrupulously, in the 'pseudo-memoirs' of Madame d'Epinay).

Considering how much else there is in the *Confessions* besides self-justification, it is a pity that he began the work as he did. Many readers have been turned away from it by the apparently self-righteous final sentence of the introduction: 'Let each of them in turn reveal his heart at the feet of your throne with the same sincerity, and then let a single one of them say to you, if he dare: I was better than that man' (I, 5). This strident sentence was written at the height of Rousseau's persecution mania, when he believed he was being represented as a monster. He therefore characteristically carries the battle into the enemy camp, using the hyperbole which comes naturally to him. It is important, however, to note exactly what he is saying. The *Discourse on Inequality* distinguishes firmly between goodness (lack of malice) and virtue (self-denying action for the good of others). At this point at least, he is only laying claim to the former.

Be that as it may, the effect of this brutal challenge is strong and unfortunate. It suggests moreover that the counsel for the defence can easily become a prosecutor, like the 'judge penitent' in Camus's novel *The Fall*. Contemporaries claimed that Rousseau admitted his own crimes so as to render more credible his attacks on others. He himself said on several occasions that in confessing himself he was bound to confess others, to reveal their failings as well as his own. He believed himself to be free of malice and claimed that there was no personal satire in the *Confessions*, but anyone reading the portrait of Grimm (see below, pp. 55–6), cannot fail to be struck by its ferocity. Such vindictiveness was precisely what Hume, Diderot and others had feared, and it was unduly stressed by early commentators. In fact, it occupies a relatively small place in the work as a whole.

Confession, self-defence and aggression are all acts designed to alter one's relations with others. Rousseau's third main aim, self-knowledge, can lay claim to greater disinterestedness. He thought he was doing humanity a service by presenting a true picture of his inner self; his autobiography was not to be an 'ordinary life, disguised and whitewashed' (*Corr.* XXV, 189), but a uniquely frank disclosure. At several points in the text he returns to this desire to tell the truth about his inner life, but the clearest statement of all is contained in the Neuchâtel preamble (I, 1148–55). This important text does not figure in the final version of the *Confessions*, and it is worth presenting it here in some detail.

Rousseau begins by observing that even those who claim to know human nature tend to know only themselves and to use themselves as their models for understanding other people. As a result we are constantly misinterpreting one another. He has decided therefore 'to enable my readers to make a step forward in the knowledge of men' by offering them a true picture of another person, 'and this person will be myself'. His self-portrait will be a 'point of comparison', helping others to know and judge both themselves and others. For such purposes most existing biographies are inadequate, since they are merely 'ingenious novels' in which a person's actions and words are fitted together according to some neat psychological scheme. On the contrary, for real knowledge of others, we need to 'distinguish their acquired traits from their original nature, to see how their character was formed, what circumstances developed it, what succession [*enchaînement*] of secret feelings made it what it now is, and how it was modified so as to produce the most contradictory and unexpected results'. All this, says Rousseau, is known only to the person in question: 'No one can write a man's life but himself.' And even then, the chances are that he will put on a mask, writing an apologia rather than a biography.

Rousseau's aim, therefore, is to provide for the first time a complete account, 'to show myself in my entirety to the public', to 'say everything'. It will be an honest account, and this will distinguish him from Michel de Montaigne, author of the *Essays*, who is described as one of 'the falsely sincere people who aim to deceive by telling the truth'. While there may be some truth in this charge, it hardly does justice to Montaigne, who is the prime example of this kind of psychological enquiry into the self and probably the greatest influence on Rousseau's own self-scrutiny. What is more, the accusation is one that would constantly backfire: Rousseau's conviction that he knew himself was not one that persuaded all readers; Hume for instance wrote of him in 1766: 'Nobody knows himself less.' Reflecting later on problems of self-knowledge in the fourth of the *Reveries* Rousseau concluded that 'the KNOW THYSELF of the temple of Delphi was not so easy a maxim to follow as I had thought in my *Confessions*' (I, 1024). In the earlier book, however, although he is sometimes puzzled, he generally seems to believe that he does understand his inner life; 'I feel my heart', he writes on the first page. What is more, he claims in the Neuchâtel text that it is in his interest not to disguise the truth, since his name is likely to go down to posterity and 'I would prefer to be known as I really am, with all my faults, rather than as someone with imaginary virtues who is not me.'

This quotation suggests that we are not dealing with some purely disinterested scientific enterprise, but the stance of the dispassionate observer is certainly an important element in Rousseau's autobiographical writing. He shares with his reader his surprise at the 'bizarre' things he has done and tries to offer true psychological explanations, unearthing 'the deepest seeds of my secret passions' (as he puts it in the first draft of the spanking scene at Bossey (I, 1156)), exploring the secret *enchaînement* of his feelings and showing how they were shaped by his changing environment. The dominant philosophy in Paris at this time was the 'sensationalism' that explained human ideas and feelings fundamentally as the result of the combination of sense impressions. Rousseau was sufficiently influenced by such theories to have planned a book called the *Ethics of the Senses* (*La Morale sensitive*). The project is described in Book 9 of the *Confessions*; it was never executed, but one can reasonably regard some passages in the autobiography as contributions to this sort of knowledge. This is how the attention given to apparently 'puerile' details is justified at the end of Book 4:

There is a certain succession of affections and ideas which modify those that follow them and which one needs to know to be able to judge them properly. I seek everywhere to show clearly the first causes so as to explain the resulting chain of effects. I would wish in some way to make my soul transparent to the reader's eyes, and to that end I seek to show him it from every point of view, to display it in every possible light, to proceed in such a way that he does not miss a single movement in it, so that he can judge for himself the principle that produces them.   (I, 174–5)

In other words, the author is the observer who provides the data; it is we, the readers, who have the task of interpreting and judging.

Rousseau's fourth main motive is less openly declared in the Neuchâtel preamble, but recurs constantly in the text of the *Confessions*. He is writing for his own pleasure. First of all, there is the familiar pleasure of reliving moments of former happiness. Notice the movement between past and present in the following passage, evoking his return to Chambéry, where he expects to see Madame de Warens (or 'Maman') after a long absence: 'In writing about my travels I am as I was when travelling; I cannot bear to arrive. My heart was beating with joy as I approached my dear Maman; and this did not make me go any more quickly. I like walking at my own pace, stopping when I choose' (I, 172). So at various points in his narrative, the author slows down to savour the satisfaction of recalling 'puerile' details, even at the risk of annoying his readers. In fact these pleasant backwaters are one of the main attractions of the book for many people today.

In some notes intended for a self-portrait, Rousseau once wrote: 'Readers, I enjoy thinking about myself, and I write as I think' (I, 1120). This is not mere vanity. All his 'art of enjoyment' (to use another of his titles) is based on finding satisfaction in one's own existence. That does not have to mean *writing* about it, of course. Recounting the long walks of his youth, he notes with regret that he never wrote down all the thoughts that filled his mind: 'Ten volumes a day would not have been enough'. But he answers himself: 'Why write . . .? Why sacrifice the charm of present enjoyment so as to tell others that I had enjoyed myself?' (I, 162). Speaking of present pleasure this may be true, but the *Confessions* are the book of a man of fifty or more, whose present existence was far from joyful. By recreating his former existence in a lasting and satisfying form, he was able to double his present being. Just as in his expansive daydreams he conjured up 'beings after my own heart', so in writing his memoirs he remembers – and partly creates – a Jean-Jacques after his own heart, a younger man who for all his faults can reassure the older man by his goodness and gladden him with his triumphs. Unlike the autobiographer who writes out of self-disgust, Rousseau wants to be happy with himself, to comfort himself.

Think for instance of Book 6 and the idyll of Les Charmettes, the 'peaceful but rapid moments which have given me the right to say I have lived' (I, 225). Rousseau wrote these pages, as far as we know, in the summer of 1767, at Trye, where he was recovering from the distress of the Hume affair and the flight from England. The younger self who emerges from his past brings the much-needed certainty that at heart he is a good, innocent creature, worthy of the joys of paradise. Whether he actually achieved happiness in this way at Trye we cannot know. The reiteration of the words 'and I was happy' in the second paragraph of Book 6 might suggest an anguished attempt to conjure up happiness quite as much as a successful return to a remembered Eden. What he says is mixed: 'these memories of the time I am speaking of, so vivid and so true, often make me happy in spite of my misfortunes' (I, 226).

At all events, it is evident that one of Rousseau's main motives in writing his own life was the satisfaction of personal desire. Sometimes this desire was partly or wholly unconscious. We do not know what went on in his conscious mind as he wrote the long account of his masochistic sexual inclinations in Book 1, but to the modern reader it seems likely that this was a 'dark and miry labyrinth' (I, 18) that attracted him. The desires he felt when spanked by Mademoiselle Lambercier correspond to permanent inclinations which had to remain unsatisfied in reality, but could be satisfied in the imagination of the writer. He admits that, like an 'old madman', he remembers all too clearly the face of little Mademoiselle Goton who treated him 'like a schoolmistress' (I, 27).

I have dwelt on four fundamental impulses or aims. No doubt there are others (for instance the desire to create something which will please his readers aesthetically and win their applause), but the four I have indicated are the ones which emerge most clearly from a reading of Rousseau's text and the accompanying documents. All of them are important; no single one of them is always dominant. The balance changes from book to book. Confession of faults is more in evidence in the early books, which reveal aspects of his life that few readers knew about. Self-justification and aggression reach a peak in Book 9 and are generally more prominent in Part II, written with the public readings in mind. Psychological investigation is more important in the sections devoted to childhood and adolescence, since this is where he explains the origins of his adult character. The writer's own pleasure surfaces throughout the book; if one is more aware of it in the early books, this may be because of the subject matter, or because of the easier conditions in which these books were written. But all these aims are present in all twelve books, and all may be present on a single page.

Chapter 3

Structure, form and language

The *Confessions* is a long book and not particularly easy to grasp in its entirety. As is the case with most autobiographies, its overall structure is a chronological line; it begins with the hero's birth and follows his life through its many vicissitudes until he reaches old age. In this respect, autobiography is like other life stories, such as biography and a certain type of novel. The *Confessions*, in particular, possess the structure of the 'memoir novel' which was popular in the eighteenth century. In such works the hero, usually from the vantage point of mature wisdom, retraces his or her steps through adventure, crime and disaster. Rousseau's book contains allusions to some of these, which may have served him as models: Defoe's *Robinson Crusoe* (1719), one of his favourite books, Lesage's *Gil Blas* (1715–35), an entertaining narrative of successful ambition, Prévost's *Cleveland* (1731), an immense fresco of passion and adventure which left its mark on the young Jean-Jacques, and the *Confessions of the Count of* *** (1741), a story of worldly vice and conversion by his friend Duclos.

Like such narratives, and unlike most biographies and many of the novels which take the form of a biography (e.g. Stendhal's *The Scarlet and the Black*), autobiography is bound to be in a sense unfinished. The end of life is death, which is excluded here. Nevertheless in novels such as the *Confessions of the Count of* ***, the standpoint of maturity does allow the author to steer his hero into port after the shipwrecks and storms of his or her younger life. Likewise authors of autobiographies, far from being content with a mere chronicle of 'the story so far', often seek to impose a sense of completion on their text, to reveal in the life a shape which makes sense of the whole sequence of events. This is what Roy Pascal, in his important book, *Design and Truth in Autobiography* (1960), described as the 'design' essential to success in the genre.

As the last chapter suggested, when Rousseau wrote his life story he was not simply aiming for an entertaining chronicle of the *Gil Blas* variety. He aimed to present a meaningful image of his own character and destiny. I shall attempt in the next chapter to bring out more fully the significance he attached to his biography and to show how he created a more or less coherent self-portrait out of the chaos of events offered by his life. But such a vision is intimately bound up with the structure he gives to his narrative and the way he writes, and these are the subject of the present chapter.

Structure

If autobiographies are all unfinished, then it must be said that the *Confessions* are more so than most. Rousseau originally intended to write a third part, taking the story up to 1770, but he gave this up, just as he abandoned any idea of reworking Part II. The text we have finishes, not with some crowning achievement or the discovery of a final resting place, but with the hero thrust into new adventures. What these will be is hinted at darkly, but was never to be told in full by Rousseau. Nor are the *Confessions* simply unfinished; the author emphasises as he approaches the end that he is losing the thread:

The further I go in my story, the less I can give it any order or sequence. The agitation of my subsequent life has not allowed events sufficient time to arrange themselves in my mind. They have been too numerous, too varied, too unpleasant to be narrated without confusion.   (I, 622)

Like Kafka's *Castle*, his life story seems to lose itself in a dark labyrinth. In this respect at least, it is at the opposite remove from the autobiography of the mature man who has accomplished his life's work and can look back on his past with the superior vision of retirement. This is no doubt partly due to the difficult circumstances of writing, but one notes too that Rousseau left several works unfinished, and that by his own account (in Book 3) he found composition difficult. In particular the classical art of transitions did not come easily to him. It seems probable that much of the work was drafted in separate sections that had then to be stitched together into a single whole, so it is not surprising if it is not always easy to perceive a clear structure other than a roughly chronological sequence of events. Nevertheless, if one looks carefully, certain shaping principles emerge.

To start with the most superficial, there is the division into two parts. Rousseau himself indicates how these relate to each other at the beginning of Part II (Book 7). The first part concerns his 'peaceful youth', during which he lived the modest life for which he feels himself to have been born; the second part, by contrast, will show his nature at odds with the situations into which fate has led him. The turning point is the departure for Paris in 1742. In fact the division is not as clear-cut as he suggests. He hesitated about the placing of the material of Book 7, and one could argue that the essential turning point is really the fateful vision on the road to Vincennes. Certainly Book 8 opens with one of Rousseau's portentous new beginnings – the 'first origin' of 'the long chain of my misfortunes'. So while Part II is different in tone and substance from Part I, the difference is not so absolute as the first paragraphs of Book 7 imply.

More important is the division into twelve books (a satisfying number in itself). How far can one see each book as a separate unit, capable (like the chapters of certain novels) of being summed up in a title? Book 1 is clearly 'Childhood'. It is contained between the hero's birth and his departure from Geneva at the age of fifteen. As well as giving the reader many of the 'keys' or 'seeds' which explain his later behaviour, it tells a coherent story of decline and fall (and partial recovery); it is the most carefully constructed of all twelve books. The three which follow can be seen as a single unit; this is clearly marked by the important retrospective comments at the end of Book 4. Taken together they could be called 'Wanderjahre', covering as they do the three-and-a-half nomadic, adolescent years between leaving Geneva and settling in Chambéry. Here we see the young hero walking from town to town, from job to job, from house to house, searching for a position or purpose in life. Books 2 and 3 are balanced between Annecy and Turin, between the redemptive figure of Madame de Warens and the degradation of the errant Jean-Jacques. The former takes us from a light-hearted departure to a shameful confession and is mainly devoted to Turin. The latter begins in Turin and ends, again shamefully, in Lyon, but it centres on 'Maman'. Book 4, which stretches from the moment when Jean-Jacques discovers that she has gone away to the moment when he returns to her, is above all the book of the young hero's picaresque adventures. Books 5 and 6 are also a unit, essen-tially concerned with his life with Madame de Warens, the years of relative stability which in his view revealed to him his true nature. There is some overlap between the two books, but Book 6 is more specifically the book of Les Charmettes, the paradise found, then lost.

Book 7 may be entitled 'Ambition'; it shows the author's attempts between 1742 and 1749 to make his way in the world, to gain protectors and to win fame through music. It is dominated by the story of his brief diplomatic career in Venice, but in contrast with this it also tells of the beginning of his lasting liaison with Thérèse Levasseur. After 'Ambi-tion' comes 'Success': Book 8 shows Jean-Jacques at last achieving worldly fame, the summit being the court perfor-mance of his opera, but paradoxically this is also the book of 'Conversion' and tells of the hero's personal reform, his renunciation of the world he has just conquered. Both of these books are longer than those of Part I, but the longest of all is Book 9, which we can call 'The Hermitage'. Of all the books other than Book 1 this is the most complete in itself, a tragedy which moves inexorably from the blissful springtime installation at the country house provided by Madame d'Epinay, through the writing of *La Nouvelle Héloïse* and the fateful love for Madame d'Houdetot, to the break with the *philosophes* and the departure into the snow and ice. After this, Book 10 is devoted to the hero's 'Recovery', a new beginning, and the peak of his social success, as he becomes the friend of the illustrious Maréchal and Maréchale de Luxembourg. There are forebodings here of trouble to come, and in fact this book runs over almost without a break into Book 11, which we might entitle 'Disaster'; here the unwary hero is suddenly brought down from success to banishment. And finally Book 12 is the book of 'Exile', a fitful narrative which reaches a brief resting place on the Island of Saint-Pierre before setting off again into the ominous future.

This exercise in labelling is only partly convincing, it has to be said. Rousseau did not himself give titles to the different books, and at times the division into books seems pretty arbitrary. But what sort of overall picture do the twelve books compose when read in sequence? There are, I think, at least three different ways in which we can structure the *Confessions* as a whole. In the first place, it is a story of decline and fall. Driven by his destiny, the innocent hero is gradually stripped of his illusions, expelled from his native place, corrupted by his experiences, frustrated in love, disappointed by friends, and finally exiled and driven from place to place in solitary suffering. Alternatively, the book can be seen as a succession of losses followed by partial recoveries, followed in their turn by further losses. After the disaster of Book 1 the hero wanders and searches until he regains his true place in Books 5 and 6; then comes a further fall, a second period of searching and a second recovery in Book 9. This is immediately followed by disaster, but again the hero begins a new life (with the Luxembourgs), only to be brought down again and sent off on further wanderings. Very briefly, at the end of Book 12, he seems to have reached his desired haven, but once more he is driven out into the worst of exiles, England.

Both of these accounts insist, as Rousseau intended, on the tragic nature of the work, but it would be wrong to ignore another structure that works the other way. Seen in this light, the *Confessions* is a story of achievement, in which the

successive books mark in their different ways the hero's con-
quest of a position in the world, the achievement of fame and
moral autonomy. The apprentice boy of Book 1 becomes by
turns (and with some false starts) government employee,
musician, diplomatic secretary and then, in the apotheosis of
Book 8, the writer and composer who is one of the most
celebrated men in Europe. In Book 1 he is the slave of
Ducommun, in Book 11 he plays host to Conti. And the fee-
ble wayward individual of Part I acquires in adversity virtues
worthy of the heroes he admired as a boy. None of these three
schemes is in itself sufficient to provide a single dominant
structure to the narrative, but in their interplay they suggest
a complex view of the hero's destiny which is not, as we shall
see in the next chapter, very different from that attributed to
humanity at large in Rousseau's earlier writings.

As for the structuring of the individual books, there is a
world of difference between the chaotic succession of Book
12 (which could be seen as expressing the loss of direction of
the hero's life after 1762) and the clear outlines of Book 1.
The latter has been described as a sort of overture, which
rehearses in miniature the themes and structures of the whole
work. A closer analysis, such as that proposed by Philippe
Lejeune in *Le Pacte autobiographique*, shows how carefully
Rousseau has selected and arranged his material here.

The story, complete in itself, of a boy's growing-up in
Geneva, is doubly framed. The book opens and closes with
dramatic references to the situation of the person writing; the
introduction defies his enemies and the final three lines hint
at the misfortunes to come. Immediately inside this frame
comes a second, quite different one, a double idyll. The
idealised account of the true love of Jean-Jacques's parents
(as it is recreated in the imagination of their son) is echoed in
the more overtly fictitious account of the simple and honest
life he might have led in Geneva had circumstances been different; this closes the circle and evokes a reassuring image of
changeless continuity. Inside *this* frame, however, there is a
clearly delineated succession of four sequences, correspond-
ing roughly to the four ages of man or the four ages of

childhood described in *Emile*, and these show the change and degeneration of the hero. First comes the intimate domestic life of the first ten years, dominated by the maternal figure of Aunt Suzanne, the incarnation of music; then the rural paradise of Bossey, the place of friendship, but also of the disquieting discoveries of sex and injustice; then a briefer and rather ambiguous interlude recounting the hero's return to Geneva; and finally, at greater length, his plunge into the servitude and degradation of apprenticeship, culminating in his exclusion from Geneva.

For the period of nearly sixteen years covered in this book, Rousseau obviously had to select his material. He mentions in the fourth of the *Reveries* two episodes which he decided not to use in the third of the sections indicated above; likewise there were many 'little anecdotes' which he says he would have liked to tell about the period of his schooling in Bossey, but which he sacrifices, ostensibly so as not to annoy his readers, but also so as to preserve the harmonious composition of this sequence – for the different parts are as carefully composed as the book as a whole. This is particularly true of the Bossey section. It opens with two idyllic pages evoking in general terms the 'simplicity of this rural life', Jean-Jacques's perfect friendship with his cousin and his loving relations with the Lamberciers. Then two symmetrical developments, each devoted to a scene of punishment, show the loss of this paradise (Rousseau's own image): he makes his first acquaintance with masochistic pleasure and is sent to sleep in a different room from Mademoiselle Lambercier; he is wrongly accused of breaking a comb and is beaten by his uncle. In both of these sub-sections, the particular scene, while constituting an important turning point, is also used to introduce the reader to crucial features of the hero's character. The section does not end here however; in the pages that follow, Rousseau inverts the chronological order and momentarily reestablishes the lost paradise, first with an extraordinary evocation of little details of everyday life (the barometer, the raspberry bushes, the bird flying in through the window), then with two humorous anecdotes. The first of these, very briefly told, concerns 'Mademoiselle Lambercier's behind' and echoes the earlier spanking scene, while the elaborately told story of the aqueduct is a humorous reversal of the broken-comb episode. The tone of these two stories is happy, and in this way Rousseau completes the Bossey section as a self-contained symmetrical unit, setting the two stories of degradation within scenes of innocence and balancing the movement of decline by a compensatory recovery.

This type of symmetry or equilibrium is in fact a feature of Book 1 in general. Not only is the whole story of decline placed within an idyllic frame, but in each section misfortune is set against recovery. The mother's death and the child's ailments are quickly offset by the discovery of the magic world of literature, and this is echoed at the end of the book where the adolescent takes refuge from his degrading apprentice life in the creations of his imagination. In the same way the brief but disquieting paragraph about the elder brother is immediately followed by the evocation of Aunt Suzanne and her singing. Each section of the downward path ends with loss or disaster − the mother's death, the father's departure, the loss of innocence, Mademoiselle Vulson's betrayal, the exclusion from Geneva − but all are balanced by indications of a new beginning, so that it is not surprising if at the beginning of Book 2 the catastrophic expulsion has become a buoyant departure. This structural feature emphasises the dialectic of change and continuity which is central to the *Confessions*.

Book 1 lends itself to such analysis more easily than some of the other books, but in almost all of them one can see similar principles of symmetry, contrast and gradation. Episodes are juxtaposed not only for variety (as in the very lively Book 4), but above all to create a series of oppositions, light and shade, comedy and drama, happiness and misery − as in the violent ups and downs of Books 2 and 3 or the strong contrast between the joyful opening and the ensuing disaster in Books 6 and 9. The books almost all begin and end in a striking way, often with a new departure and a scene of humiliation or expulsion respectively, and this fairly obvious point may alert us to other echoes which are set up from one book to another, helping to unify the work as a whole. Such echoes may involve resemblance or contrast, the former showing the recurrence of constant patterns of behaviour or feeling, the latter pointing up some irreversible change, for better or worse.

Perhaps the clearest example of significant contrast is that between the grotesque concert in Lausanne (Book 4) and the performance of *The Village Soothsayer* (Book 8). In recounting each episode, Rousseau refers to the other, so that the reader is made conscious of the remarkable rise in the world of the crazy young man of Lausanne. Similar oppositions are set up between the experience as a servant in Turin (Book 2) and as ambassador's secretary in Venice (Book 7) or, less happily, between the scene in the cherry orchard at Toune (Book 4) and that in the garden with Madame d'Houdetot (Book 9). And more generally we are encouraged to juxtapose and compare the different love affairs (from Mademoiselle Vulson to Madame d'Houdetot) or the behaviour of the different benefactors (from Madame de Warens to Madame d'Epinay). As for the scenes which resemble one another, against the scenes of expulsion already mentioned can be set the recurrent image of a self-contained rural paradise in which Jean-Jacques can find and find again his true nature. A clear line takes one from Bossey (Book 1) to Les Charmettes (Book 6) and to the Hermitage (Book 9). In Part II, as the hero finds the world increasingly hostile, an interesting variant emerges – the island. In Book 7 there is the brief confinement in the leper house at Genoa, where Rousseau compares himself to Robinson Crusoe, and there is a passing mention of the Borromean Islands. The latter is picked up in Book 9 (as a possible setting for *La Nouvelle Héloïse*) and again in Book 10 in the description of the 'little chateau' where Jean-Jacques is housed by the Maréchal de Luxembourg; this 'appears absolutely surrounded by water', like 'an enchanted island, or the prettiest of the three Borromean Islands' (I, 521). And finally comes the real island, the Island of Saint-Pierre in Book 12, a scene which was later more fully developed in one of Rousseau's most beautiful texts, the fifth of the *Reveries*. Such echoes − and there are many more − set up networks of signification which will be explored in the next chapter.

Narrative form

The *Confessions* can thus be compared to a novel as a structured work of art. They also share with prose fiction the use of various narrative procedures. The basic mode of story-telling is of course first-person retrospective narration ('I was born in Geneva in 1712 . . .'). This is interspersed with other modes. From time to time, for instance, we encounter apostrophes − to God, to Madame de Warens, to Aunt Suzanne, to the 'precious moments' of Les Charmettes, and so on. But much more importantly there is the continual address to the reader. On almost every page, Rousseau interrupts his *narrative* with what modern criticism calls *discourse*, in which the past tenses of story-telling typically give way to the present tense of discussion and reflexion. He reasons or jokes with the reader, defying us to find him guilty, appealing to our common sense or experience, sharing our incredulity, playing with our expectations. Or else he may simply talk quietly about himself:

Flat country, however beautiful, has never seemed so to me. I need torrents, rocks, fir trees, dark woods, mountains, rugged paths to climb up and down, precipices by my side to make me really frightened.   (I, 172)

As he writes these lines with gentle self-mockery, Rousseau has moved away from the moment he is describing (the walk from Lyon to Chambéry) and is talking about his constant taste at all ages. The present joins hands with the past. For the distinction between narrative and discourse points us to an essential element in autobiography, one of which Rousseau was rightly conscious, the coming together of different periods of time. This is how he puts it in the Neuchâtel preamble: 'By giving myself over at the same time to the memory of the impression received and to my present feeling,

I shall give a double picture of the state of my soul, as it was when the event occurred and as it is when I describe it' (I, 1154). The narrator of the present (and one must remember that this 'present' extends from 1756 to 1770) is superimposed on the main character. Both are named by the same pronoun, 'I', but in a typical sentence such as the following, this 'I' refers to different people: 'If I had been young and attractive and if Madame d'Houdetot had subsequently been weak, I should blame her conduct now' (I, 441). As this example shows, the relation between 'I' the character and 'I' the narrator can be one of distance – the distance of shame or judgement, or frequently that of mockery and irony. Equally it may be a relation of closeness, in which the present seems to fuse with the past. There is no end to the possible permutations, and herein lies much of the fascination of the *Confesions*. One could argue indeed that the past-tense narrative is in the last resort subordinate to the discursive voice of the present. In reading Rousseau's autobiography one is not so much following the story of his life as listening to him as he creates it and reflects on his own creation.

In addition to the voices of narration and discourse, two other elements need to be mentioned. The first is the authentic written document incorporated into the text – in particular the many letters which swell Book 9. These often create an interesting discord, for the document may not seem to fit the author's commentary, as for instance Diderot's letter of 1757 (Book 9, p. 476) and Rousseau's violent reaction. The second is quite different: this is the inclusion of what purports to be a record of words actually spoken by the characters. These are sometimes brief and striking – 'an aqueduct!' – and seem to spring out of the past with special authenticity. Or they may work the other way. Thus when Rousseau recalls his eloquent speech to Madame de Warens in Book 6, the fictional nature of autobiography suddenly becomes more apparent:

'No, Maman', I said to her with passion, 'I love you too much to
wish to debase you; your possession is too precious for me to share
it; the regrets which accompanied it when I obtained it have grown
with my love; no, I cannot keep it at the same price. You will always
have my adoration; be worthy of it always; it is still more necessary
for me to honour you than to possess you.'   (I, 264)

Elaborate dialogue can pass as real in an avowed novel, but
it undermines the pretension to reality of an autobiography.

In a work setting out to recover time past, another essential
formal feature is the management of chronology. The narrative of the *Confessions* is basically linear but far from
straightforwardly so. The order of presentation is disturbed
in various ways, the most important figures here being
flashback and *anticipation*, both of which may bring together
widely distant moments in time. Flashbacks may be attributed
to the narrator, who interrupts the story to take the reader
back to previous happenings which explain the present; in
Books 2 and 3 the brief history of Madame de Warens's
earlier life helps us understand her in something like the way
we understand the hero. Or else the flashback may occur in
the hero's mind, as in Book 9, where his new found rural
freedom makes Jean-Jacques dream of his younger days:
'Soon I saw gathered around me all the objects of my
youthful emotions: Mademoiselle Galley, Mademoiselle de
Graffenried, Mademoiselle de Breil, Madame Basile,
Madame de Larnage, my pretty pupils, and even the seductive
Zulietta, whom my heart cannot forget' (I, 427). In one
sentence the time of Book 9 is joined with that of Books 2,
3, 4, 5, 6 and 7, as well as the time of narration (in the con-
cluding clause).

Anticipation is even more important, for the whole of
Rousseau's story is told in the light of later developments.
The child is father to the man, so the narrator, having
described his first thefts in Book 1, moves by way of a discussion of his character to an anecdote (the visit to the Opera
with Francueil) whose 'proper' place would be Book 7 or 8.
There are more ominous types of anticipation, notably
dramatic irony, where narrator and reader share knowledge

of what awaits the unknowing hero, and suspense, in which the reader too is kept in the dark, while the narrator speaks cryptically of disasters still to come. This last figure recurs throughout the *Confessions*; the ending of Book 1, with its foreboding of 'the miseries of my life' is echoed by the brief announcement at the end of Book 12 of a tragic sequel.

As well as changing the order of events, a narrator can vary the *tempo*, moving from detailed scene to rapid summary. If Book 1 covers fifteen years, Book 2 devotes the same number of pages to six months. The eighteen months between the return to Geneva and the move to the Hermitage are given a few pages at the end of Book 8; the roughly similar time spent at the Hermitage occupies about fifteen times the space in the following book. A slower tempo generally underlines the importance of an episode; thus the Venetian interlude and the performance of *The Village Soothsayer* are both given the honours of detailed treatment.

In fact Rousseau often changes tempo in a disconcerting way, swinging rapidly from a concentration on particularly important moments in his life to a broad view of his destiny. Look for instance at the opening pages of Book 8, which tell of the fateful vision on the road to Vincennes. If one studies these pages in some detail, one sees not only the normal changes of tempo that any story-teller uses almost automatically, but also the surprising absence of what one might have expected, a full-scale evocation of the half-hour which changed the author's life. Why is this? Rousseau himself explains that since he had described this scene in a letter to Malesherbes in 1762, he had forgotten the details because to record a scene in writing was to obliterate it from his memory. But considering that he could well have re-used his earlier description, this does not seem a very convincing explanation of the very brief treatment of this crucial scene. I would suggest rather that in 1769–70 (when these pages were written) he was no longer as anxious as in 1762 to dwell on a moment which he now saw even more blackly as the beginning of his misfortunes, and was more concerned to shift the blame on to others. Book 8 was written when his mind was full of the 'conspiracy' — and one notes that the two brief 'scenes' which do occur in these pages both involve a person involved in the so-called plot, his friend Diderot. In the first the reader is shown the selfishness with which the imprisoned *philosophe* receives Rousseau's heart-felt sympathy; the second tells how Diderot pushed him to take the path which would lead to his ruin: 'He exhorted me to develop my ideas and compete for the prize. I did so and from that instant I was lost. All the rest of my life and my misfortunes were the inevitable result of that moment of madness' (I, 351). Diderot's fateful role in Rousseau's destiny is stressed both by the two brief scenes and by the subsequent withdrawal from close-up to a long shot encompassing the rest of the author's life. The basic point to emerge from such considerations is therefore that narrative form is not a matter of indifference. It is always worth looking carefully at the way Rousseau tells his story; his emphases, his gaps and his shifting point of view can all tell the reader a lot about his conscious or unconscious aims in writing.

Language

The author of the *Confessions* had an extraordinary reputation for eloquence among his contemporaries. Many of those who detested his principles spoke admiringly of his way with words. This could be a double-edged compliment. To praise his style might mean to deny the value of his ideas, implying that he was a hypocrite, a master of rhetoric who did not believe a word of what he said. He was therefore driven (like many orators) to present himself as a simple person writing out of the conviction of his heart. In so far as this simplicity might lead him to shock the taste of the polite reading public, this could only be a proof of his sincerity. And this could of course in turn become a more sophisticated form of eloquence — the eloquence that denies eloquence. Rousseau notes in Book 9 of the *Confessions* (I, 403) that his books sold well precisely because he did not aim to please an audience. The writer remains a writer, however much he may protest.

Autobiographical writing presents special problems for a writer concerned with authenticity. In telling the story of his life, Rousseau knew that he was also exposing his state of mind at the time of writing, and this above all dictated the kind of style he had to adopt. Once again it is the Neuchâtel preamble which best expresses his views:

> To say what I have to say, I would need to invent a language as new as my project; for what tone, what style would allow me to unravel the immense chaos of feelings that kept me so constantly agitated, feelings so various, so contradictory, so vile often, and sometimes so sublime? (I, 1153)

After speaking of the particular difficulties posed by the 'revolting, indecent, puerile and often ridiculous details' he would have to depict, he goes on:

> If I choose to write a carefully composed book as others do, I shall not be painting myself, but putting on greasepaint. What I am engaged on is a portrait, not a book. I shall be working, so to speak, in a *camera obscura*. All my art will be to follow exactly the lines I see traced there. I am therefore adopting the same position on style as on subject matter. I shall not try to make it uniform, I shall change as I fancy, without scruple, I shall say everything the way I feel it or see it, not letting myself be worried by incongruity [*bigarrure*]. . . My uneven and natural style, alternately rapid and long-winded, sensible and foolish, serious and light-hearted, will itself be part of my subject. (I, 1154)

It is a typical Rousseau combination of brilliant insight and illusion. The insight concerns the crucial importance of language in autobiography, comparable to the creation of character through speech in the theatre. Illusion intrudes with the idea of reproducing the workings of the mind on paper without self-censureship or control. We see here one of Rousseau's central fantasies, that of making himself 'transparent' to others. Jean Starobinski has worked out the implications of this in his remarkable book *Jean-Jacques Rousseau, la transparence et l'obstacle*, showing how he strives for a utopian state of unmediated communication. Language is inescapably a medium, and transparency between souls a dream, but the search for the impossible did at least lead Rousseau to a radically new way of writing. In language as much as anything else, the *Confessions* are a landmark in French literature.

The word *bigarrure* is perhaps the key. As against classical canons of unity of tone, Rousseau welcomes variety and contrast, and this not in a basically playful or comic book (where it would be acceptable) but in an enterprise of the greatest seriousness. The *Confessions* do indeed speak in several voices, not just from book to book, but often on a single page. One may broadly distinguish a certain number of types of writing: passionate eloquence with a tendency to exaggeration, business-like narrative, sharp satire, picturesque description, irony and humour, lyrical evocation of states of real or imagined happiness. Certain of these predominate more in particular sections of the work: humour and evocation towards the beginning, eloquence and satire later on.

I want now to look in some detail at the way Rousseau writes in two brief passages, from Part I and Part II respectively. As well as being very different from each other, both also contain something of the *bigarrure* which their author speaks of in the Neuchâtel preamble. One can sense in the writing his changing moods and the coexistence of the different aims I outlined in the last chapter. The first passage is from Book 1, very near the beginning; it comes directly after the solitary paragraph devoted to Rousseau's elder brother (whose role in his development was very likely more important than he himself suggests):

Si ce pauvre garçon fut élevé négligemment, il n'en fut pas ainsi de son frère, et les enfants des rois ne sauraient être soignés avec plus de zèle que je le fus durant mes premiers ans, idolâtré de tout ce qui m'environnait, et toujours, ce qui est bien plus rare, traité en enfant chéri, jamais en enfant gâté. Jamais une seule fois, jusqu'à ma sortie de la maison paternelle, on ne m'a laissé courir seul dans la rue avec les autres enfants, jamais on n'eut à réprimer en moi ni à satisfaire aucune de ces fantasques humeurs qu'on impute à la nature, et qui naissent toutes de la seule éducation. J'avais les défauts de mon âge; j'étais babillard, gourmand, quelquefois menteur. J'aurais volé des fruits, des bonbons, de la mangeaille; mais jamais je n'ai pris plaisir à faire du mal, du dégât, à charger les autres, à tourmenter de pauvres animaux. Je me souviens pourtant d'avoir une fois pissé dans la marmite d'une de nos voisines, appelée Mme Clot, tandis qu'elle était au prêche. J'avoue même que ce souvenir me fait encore rire, parce que Mme Clot, bonne femme au demeurant, était bien la vieille la plus grognon que je connus de ma vie. Voilà la courte et véridique histoire de tous mes méfaits enfantins.

Comment serais-je devenu méchant, quand je n'avais sous les yeux que des exemples de douceur, et autour de moi que les meilleures gens du monde? Mon père, ma tante, ma mie, mes parents, nos amis, nos voisins, tout ce qui m'environnait ne m'obéissait pas à la vérité, mais m'aimait, et moi je les aimais de même. Mes volontés étaient si peu excitées et si peu contrariées, qu'il ne me venait pas dans l'ésprit d'en avoir. Je puis jurer que jusqu'à mon asservissement sous un maître, je n'ai pas su ce que c'était qu'une fantaisie. Hors le temps que je passais à lire ou écrire auprès de mon père, et celui où ma mie me menait promener, j'étais toujours avec ma tante, à la voir broder, à l'entendre chanter, assis ou debout à côté d'elle, et j'étais content. Son enjouement, sa douceur, sa figure agréable, m'ont laissé de si fortes impressions, que je vois encore son air, son regard, son attitude: je me souviens de ses petits propos caressants; je dirais comment elle était vêtue et coiffée, sans oublier les deux crochets que ses cheveux noirs faisaient sur ses tempes, selon la mode de ce temps-là.

If this poor boy's upbringing was neglected, the same was not true of his brother, and the children of kings could not be more zealously cared for than I was in my early years, worshipped by all who surrounded me and, what is much less common, always loved, but never spoiled. Never once until I left my father's house was I allowed out by myself to run around in the street with the other children; never was it necessary to check or satisfy in me any of those capricious moods which are attributed to nature, and which all spring from education alone. I had the faults of my age; I was a chatterbox, greedy, sometimes a liar. I would have stolen fruit, sweets, things to eat, but I never took pleasure in doing harm, damaging things, accusing others or tormenting poor animals. I do remember however once pissing in the cooking-pot of one of our neighbours called Madame Clot while she was at chapel. I even admit that this memory still makes me laugh, because Madame Clot, who was a good soul in her way, was the grumpiest old woman I have known in all my life. Such is the brief and faithful chronicle of all my childish misdeeds.

How could I have become bad, when I had only examples of kindness to gaze on and the best people in the world all around me? My father, my aunt, my nanny, my relations, our friends, our neighbours, all who surrounded me did not obey me, it is true, but they loved me; and I loved them too. My desires were so little aroused and so little frustrated that it never entered my head to have any. I can swear that until I was enslaved to a master I did not know what a whim was. Apart from the time I spend reading or writing by my father's side, and when my nanny took me out for walks, I was always with my aunt, watched her embroidering, listening to her singing, standing or sitting beside her, and I was happy. Her cheerfulness, her sweetness, her pleasant face made such a strong impression on me that I can still see her appearance, her look, her attitude; I remember the affectionate little things she said; I could describe what she wore and how she did her hair, not forgetting the two kiss-curls her black hair made on her temples, after the fashion of those days. (I, 10)

In these lines the persecuted exile with a reputation for unsociable misanthropy no doubt wants to win over the reader to a feeling of affection for himself as a good and loving child. He also wants, for his own satisfaction, to create from memory the image of a happy, safe world, where all are in harmony. It is an enclosed world, limited to a few people; the little boy does not go out to play, and his walks with the maid Jacqueline (*ma mie*) are passed over in a few words, overshadowed by the happy indoor scenes. The phrase 'tout ce qui m'environnait' occurs in a similar position in both paragraphs; the child is at the centre of a loving environment. In the first ten lines the passivity of Jean-Jacques (as if in a cradle) is emphasised by the sentences where he is represented by an object pronoun or as the subject of passive verbs. Most important for the creation of this secure atmosphere is the rhythm. Rousseau sets clauses and phrases against one another to create a rocking movement. Take the first sentence of the second paragraph: it opens with a question (the first for some pages), which sets off a new movement, but this is immediately absorbed into the two symmetrical clauses that follow. The next sentence works by accumulation, a figure of which Rousseau is fond at all times; six nouns are listed, each with its possessive pronoun (moving from 'my' to 'our' two thirds of the way through), and of the six the first three (those closest to the child) are all monosyllables in French, and the other three (less close) all have two syllables. It is as if the author was making two circles around the child, before enclosing it all in 'tout ce qui m'environnait'. Similarly for Aunt Suzanne we have 'son enjouement, sa douceur, sa figure agréable' and 'son air, son regard, son attitude', those lulling threesomes of which the French are so fond. In the first paragraph likewise the child is 'babillard, gourmand, quelquefois menteur' and might have stolen 'des fruits, des bonbons, de la mangeaille'. In all these cases the absence of the conjunction 'et' contributes to the rhythmical effect.

I have said that one phrase is repeated verbatim, something to be avoided according to the style books, but serving its purpose here; there is also the more traditional oratorical repetition ('Jamais . . . jamais . . .') and the repetition of a similar idea in different sentences (the clause about 'humeurs' is taken up in the sentence about 'volontés'). The most memorable sentence, however, is the one beginning 'Hors le temps . . .' Here two balanced clauses push the father and the maid to one side to make room for the aunt, and then a string of simple, beautifully balanced expressions leads to a comma, a pause (like an indrawn breath) and the bare statement 'et j'étais content'. The basic conjunction 'et' replaces any causal connection, as in the earlier 'et moi je les aimais de même' or the 'et j'étais heureux' used repeatedly in the second paragraph of Book 6. In its childish simplicity, this is one of Rousseau's attempts to solve the insoluble problem of describing happiness.

The use of superlatives ('les meilleures gens du monde') and of words like 'jamais' and 'toujours' contribute further to create the image of a world apart. It is an ethereal place, with no clear outlines, a dream world. This is all the more striking if one reads this passage in relation to the preceding paragraph, where we are told of very real violence, the older brother being thrashed by the father (who was by all accounts an irascible person) and the young Jean-Jacques, like a Roman hero, trying to shelter him. It is noticeable that this ne'er-do-well brother is absent from the two paragraphs we are considering; although he must have been one of the family for some of the time being recalled here, he has been expelled *from the narrative* at the end of the previous paragraph.

In his absence there is a risk of the evocation of domestic happiness becoming altogether too much of a sweet dream. This is where another element comes in, the use of physical detail. Half-way through the first paragraph, there is something of a change in the language. For a start, we now have active verbs with 'je' as the subject; the child is not just the passive object of adoration. In addition, although we are not 'in the street', there is a move to more down-to-earth vocabulary: first the series of scolding words, 'babillard, gourmand . . . menteur', then the lists of possible thefts, all very tangible and the last, 'la mangeaille', belonging to the familiar register (more so than the inadequate translation 'things to eat'). By way of negatives the vocabulary of evil enters the text: harm, damage, tormented animals. Of course Rousseau says that he did not commit such crimes, any more than he stole things (though he 'could have' done so), but the words are there − and they lead to the one aggressive act of little Jean-Jacques.

The tiny episode of Madame Clot's pot is one of the 'puerile details' which shocked early readers and for which the author feels the need to apologise from time to time. There is no apology here, however, and Rousseau increases the affront to good taste by using the vulgar or at any rate childish 'pisser'. Elsewhere he has recourse to euphemisms (for masochism and masturbation for instance), but there are numerous occasions in the *Confessions* where he prefers the simple, crude word, even when, as here, it jars with the context. Pissing in the neighbour's pot is undoubtedly a malicious act, but its childish vulgarity, the choice of words, the repetition of the proper name and the brief sketch of Madame Clot, all defuse any feeling of real aggression. The naughty child is not a bad child. This winning of sympathy is one of the functions of the humour which is so prominent in Part I; here, moreover, Rousseau underlines it by admitting that he continues to laugh at his childish misdemeanor; we are invited to join his indulgent merriment.

There is another slightly different sort of humour at work

in this first paragraph: the light irony with which Rousseau, having first written of himself in the formal third person ('son frère'), compares his lot favourably to that of princes. Such comparisons are frequent and tend to set up a comic contrast between an insignificant hero and the characters of more 'serious' history. So too the pompous tone of the last sentence of the first paragraph, like the mock-tragic style used for the anecdote of the walnut tree at Bossey later in Book 1, establishes an ironic distance between adult writer and little hero. Rousseau has just been claiming unusual innocence for himself; this declaration reduces his 'confession' to a joke and discourages the reader from searching further.

There is no humour in the second paragraph. We are not invited to laugh at Aunt Suzanne, whose touching songs will be the subject of the next paragraph. Once again the image tends to be abstract and ethereal, very different from the precise and often comic portraits of Books 2 to 4. Aunt Suzanne is a mother figure for any reader as she sits, sews and sings. Words such as 'douceur' or 'attitude' are imprecise, so that we can make up the picture as we choose. Rousseau says he can still see her and describe her clothes and hair, but he does not do so. Or not until the very end; here, as in the first paragraph, there is a move to the concrete, just one detail, but an unexpected one. She has black hair (we might have expected blond, knowing Rousseau's symbolism of hair colour) and this hair, rather than being simply curled or waving, makes little 'crochets' at the temples. Suddenly the portrait is particularised, and Aunt Suzanne is transported from the world of dream to the real world of 'those days'. In the following pages one will see an increasing use of physical detail to conjure up the past.

Combining the real and the ethereal, Rousseau has thus created a world of enclosed happiness, harmony and unusual goodness. The relations he describes are like those he imagines for his ideal child in *Emile*. And as in *Emile*, this involves another kind of language, that of argument. The incredulous reader has to be convinced of the possibility of what is shown. So in the first paragraph, one notes the move

from the particular to the general in the sentence beginning 'Jamais une seule fois . . .' 'Ces fantasques humeurs qu'on impute à la nature, et qui naissent toutes de l'éducation' – this is the language of the treatise, with the significant opposition between two abstract terms, 'nature' and 'education'. In the second paragraph, Rousseau has recourse to a rhetorical question ('Comment serais-je . . .') and then, perhaps protesting too much, to an oath ('Je puis jurer que . . .'). Thus although the dominant voice in this passage is probably that of the older man remembering (or imagining) his early childhood with an appealing mixture of nostalgia and humour, one can hear too that of the maligned philosopher, the author of the discourses and *Emile*, anxious to convince his reader not only that he was a good and affectionate child, but that such a character is the natural product of a good and affectionate environment.

After the angel, the devil. The second passage comes from a section of Book 9 devoted to Melchior Grimm. The immediate context is the growing discord between Jean-Jacques and his 'protector' Madame d'Epinay, which will lead to a final break at the end of Book 9. Rousseau attributes this largely to Grimm, who has become Madame d'Epinay's lover and treats Jean-Jacques (his elder by ten years and his former bosom companion) with open contempt:

Aussi fat qu'il était vain, avec ses gros yeux troubles et sa figure dégingandée, il avait des prétentions près des femmes, et depuis sa farce avec Mlle Fel, il passait auprès de plusieurs d'entre elles pour un homme à grands sentiments. Cela l'avait mis à la mode, et lui avait donné du goût pour la propreté de femme: il se mit à faire le beau; sa toilette devint une grande affaire; tout le monde sut qu'il mettait du blanc, et moi, qui n'en croyais rien, je commençai de le croire, non seulement par l'embellissement de son teint, et pour avoir trouvé des tasses de blanc sur sa toilette, mais sur ce qu'entrant un matin dans sa chambre je le trouvai brossant ses ongles avec une petite vergette faite exprès; ouvrage qu'il continua fièrement devant moi. Je jugeai qu'un homme qui passe deux heures tous les matins à brosser ses ongles peut bien passer quelques instants à remplir de blanc les creux de sa peau. Le bon homme Gauffecourt, qui n'était pas sac-à-diable, l'avait assez plaisamment surnommé Tyran-le-Blanc.

Tout cela n'était que des ridicules, mais bien antipathiques à mon caractère. Ils achevèrent de me rendre suspect le sien. J'eus peine à croire qu'un homme à qui la tête tournait de cette façon pût conserver un cœur bien placé. Il ne se piquait de rien tant que de sensibilité d'âme et d'énergie de sentiment. Comment cela s'accordait-il avec des défauts qui sont propres aux petites âmes? Comment les vifs et continuels élans que fait hors de lui-même un cœur sensible peuvent-ils le laisser s'occuper sans cesse de tant de petits soins pour sa petite personne? Eh! mon Dieu! celui qui sent embraser son cœur de ce feu céleste cherche à l'exhaler, et veut montrer le dedans. Il voudrait mettre son cœur sur son visage; il n'imaginera jamais d'autre fard.

As foolish as he was vain, with his big watery eyes and his gangling figure, he had set himself up as a lady's man, and ever since the farcical episode with Mademoiselle Fel several women had taken him for a man of great feeling. This had made him much sought after and given him a taste for feminine cleanliness; he started to play the beau, his toilet became a matter of great importance, it came to everyone's knowledge that he used white face powder, and I, who didn't believe a word of it at first, I came to believe it, not only from his improved complexion and from finding pots of face powder on his dressing table, but because on coming into his bedroom one morning I found him buffing his nails with a special little wand, a task which he proudly continued to my face. I concluded that a man who spends two hours every morning buffing his nails can easily spend a few moments filling the pits on his skin with face powder. Old Gauffecourt, who was no scandal-peddler, gave him the entertaining nickname of *White Tyrant*.

All these were only ridiculous foibles, but they were very antipathetic to my nature. They finally made his character suspect to me. I found it hard to believe that a man whose head was affected in this way could keep his heart in the right place. He was proud of nothing so much as his sensitive soul and strength of feeling. How could this go with faults characteristic of petty souls? How can the vigorous and continual movements which lift a sensitive heart out of itself, allow a person to spend his time unceasingly occupied with so many little cares for his little person? Good God! the man who feels his heart burning with that heavenly fire seeks to pour it forth and to show what is within him. He will want to wear his heart on his face; no other cosmetic will ever enter his mind.   (I, 467–8)

This passage, like most of Book 9, was almost certainly written at Monquin, in the dark winter of 1769–70. Rousseau was convinced as he wrote that Grimm was the first begetter

of the universal conspiracy against him, and that he was exposed to the hostile and mocking gaze of a public won over to Grimm's way of thinking. What he does here, as he comes to Grimm's part in the catastrophe that had led to his present situation, is to turn the tables on his enemy. In this text it is not Jean-Jacques who is the object of attention and derision, but Grimm. Various foolish women may consider him a man of feeling, but 'everyone' discovers that he uses face powder, and 'le bon homme Gauffecourt' (which implies the jolly familiarity suggested in 'old Gauffecourt') gives him an appropriate nickname. Rousseau can thus be (in imagination) one of a theatre audience looking with hostile amusement at the White Tyrant.

The *Confessions* contain scores of comic and even grotesque portraits, and often these bear witness to an agreable and exuberant sense of humour, for which their author is not always given credit. Here, however, the comedy is aggressive, not indulgent. In the first of these paragraphs, Rousseau does his utmost to belittle Grimm, to present him as a repellent and ridiculous figure of fun. Aunt Suzanne was a fairly ethereal figure; Grimm is very much physically present. Rousseau uses a series of trivial and disagreable words: 'gros yeux troubles', 'figure dégingandée', 'fard', 'tasses de blanc', 'petite vergette', 'creux de sa peau' − and the familiar, rather brutal tone is reinforced by the use of the popular Genevan expression 'sac-à-diable'. But he does not want simply to denigrate his enemy; he wants to gain the reader's complicity by being humorous at his expense. The end of the preceding paragraph compared Grimm to a vainglorious hero in a contemporary comedy; this mocking literary allusion is continued through the word 'farce' and the glimpses of Grimm in such roles as 'man of fashion' and 'man of feeling'. The adverb 'fièrement', grotesquely applied to the polishing of finger-nails (a process made to last for an improbable two hours), prepares for the culminating mention of 'Tyran le Blanc' − a character in a romance of chivalry. The rhythm in the earlier passage helped to build up an atmosphere of happy security, whereas here the rather unwieldy accumulation of phrases in the central sentence seems to mime the growing absurdity of the personage, who is cut down to size in the final sentence.

In all of this, Rousseau attempts to maintain the detached tone of the comic writer, the better to avenge himself on a man who had (in his view) ruined him out of envy and spite. His portrait of Grimm is memorable, unfair and cruel, and this is because it springs from a strong emotional involvement which comes into the open in the second paragraph. The notion of cosmetic (which might seem harmless enough) is connected for Rousseau with his own fear of being taken for a hypocrite, his vehement insistence that he was always sincere and genuine. It is insufferable to him that such a villanous play-actor as Grimm can be credited with good qualities while he, Grimm's victim, is seen as a monster. In the second paragraph, therefore, he abandons the portrait of his enemy and launches into general arguments whose purpose is above all to demonstrate his own goodness. The writing becomes insistent, with vigorously accentuated rhythm, rhetorical exclamations and questions, and the traditional elemental metaphors (here of heat and fire) which he often uses to describe his inner life. The subject of the paragraph is still nominally Grimm, but in the fifth sentence the tense of the verb changes in mid-sentence from the past (referring to 1757) to the generalising present. It is quite evident by this stage that the author is thinking of himself. Although he does not say so openly, the 'celui qui sent' of the sentence beginnning 'Eh! mon Dieu!' is certainly Jean-Jacques. The satirical portrait has slipped, perhaps unintentionally, into a proclamation of values, an unhumorous confrontation of the good self and the wicked other. As a result the cosmetic image, which was the starting point of this development, makes a jarring impression when it reappears at the end of the paragraph, since it is now seen against the impassioned metaphorical notion of 'wearing one's heart on one's face'.

In this passage (which is of course only a fragment of a longer sequence), one can see clearly what Rousseau meant when he said that his writing would reveal his changing feelings. More than in the passage I discussed earlier (which was probably composed at greater leisure), one can feel here the pulse of passion in the writing. In both passages, however, there are shifts and discontinuities in the style which point to the complexity of his attitude to his past. In his manner of writing he communicates a truth about himself which he would not have wished (or been able?) to state discursively. He was eloquent, certainly, but whereas some of the eloquence which his contemporaries so admired can now seem all too much like the standard rhetoric of his time, the living, changing, motley language of the *Confessions* strikes me as something quite different. Rousseau's autobiographical writing is dense and highly-charged in a way that was exceptional in his time − and since.

Chapter 4

The meaning of the story

At the end of Book 4, Rousseau places the responsibility for interpreting the *Confessions* on his reader: 'It is for him to assemble these elements and to determine the being they make up; the result must be his work, and if he is mistaken, the mistake will be his' (I, 175). One's reaction is 'yes and no': of course we are free to come to our own conclusions, but the preceding chapters have shown that Rousseau does not simply present 'the facts'; he shapes and tells his story so as it convey his own vision of things. Drawing on the lessons of his earlier books, he creates an image of the self and its relations with others which has meaning not only for himself, but for his society and for humanity at large. This does not mean that the whole work is designed to promote an ideology; as he explores the labyrinth of his past, the author is led in many directions, carried away at times by the sheer pleasure of reliving his younger days. All the time, however, he strives to make sense, for himself and for his readers, of the 'immense chaos' of his complex story. In this chapter I shall try to tease out the main threads of his own understanding of his life. Whether this account convinces the reader is another matter, to be dealt with in the next chapter. For the time being I want to present Rousseau's view of things without interposing too much by way of critical comment.

One can begin with a text that comes not from the *Confessions*, but from the *Dialogues*. Here one of the characters recalls how Lazarillo de Tormes, the hero of a Spanish picaresque novel, is displayed on fairgrounds as a sea-monster in a tank; only his head emerges from the water, and if he tries to speak he is immediately dragged under by a hidden rope. What, he asks, if some spectator had shouted to the crowd: 'You are being deceived; this supposed monster is a man' (I, 768)? So in the *Confessions* Rousseau seeks to show that he is not a 'monster such as could not even exist' (I, 645), but 'a man in all the truth of nature' (I, 5). The latter phrase, taken from the first page of the work, is by no means easy to interpret; it could mean simply that the author is painting a true portrait of himself, but it suggests also that the self he is portraying is in fact 'natural man'. And if we remember how in the *Discourse on Inequality* natural man was compared to the statue of Glaucus, disfigured by the sea and storms until he resembled a sea-monster, we can see that Rousseau is engaged here in the same exercise of digging down beneath appearances to find the true personality. We shall not be surprised if some of what he finds is the same in both works.

Natural man

In each generation, the child is a new beginning, a reminder of our true nature. It is for this reason that childhood is given such unprecedented prominence in the *Confessions*. More than this, Rousseau confesses that in later years he has remained 'an old child', not properly adapted to the adult ways of society. He possesses the rare privilege of remaining close to nature − a dubious privilege, since his natural, childish character leads people to misinterpret his behaviour. For instance, because his slowness of wit makes him shy, he has been accused of a misanthropy which is far from his true nature. With the Luxembourg family he seemed 'vile and guilty' when he was only 'foolish and embarrassed' (I, 535). This gaucherie, born of shyness, is often alluded to, generally in comic episodes, where the author can laugh indulgently at his own follies. The point is that these are not the product of the evil passions of malice, hate, envy and cruelty. Natural man is good, in the sense that he does not willingly harm other people, and Rousseau constantly insists on his own lack of malice. At the end of Book 11, noting his child-like ability to forget misfortunes and injuries, he declares: 'It is to this fortunate disposition, I feel, that I owe my freedom from the spirit of resentment which ferments in a vindictive heart' (I, 585). Similarly, the natural man of the *Discourse on Inequality* is free of self-love or vanity, and Rousseau writes of himself: 'I believe that no individual of our species was ever less vain by nature than I am' (I, 14).

Other supposedly natural qualities go to make up the picture. Some of them might be described as vices, but they too are signs of primitive innocence. Take greed, for example. Food occupies a large place in the *Confessions*; Rousseau does not disguise his pleasure in eating. What could be more natural, more attuned to the basic 'love of self' of natural man? This attachment to food has nothing to do with sophisticated gastronomy, of course. On several occasions he describes his ideal simple meal: 'With milk dishes, eggs, herbs, cheese, brown bread and decent wine, you will always be sure of giving me a treat; my good appetite will do the rest so long as I am not put off my food by a butler and lackeys standing all round me' (I, 72). The food he likes, with the exception of the wine, is often childish food − 'great bowls of milk and cream' (I, 58). In the passage analysed in the last chapter, we saw that the child is naturally greedy, and might well steal food; later on Rousseau admits to various thefts of food and drink in childhood and even in his adult years − for instance the Arbois wine stolen at the Mably household in Book 6 (I, 268–9). The vital distinction here is between stealing out of desire (as 'savages' do) and stealing out of deliberate design. In the long discussions of theft in Book 1, the author denies that he has ever been tempted to steal money. This is because money is a form of mediation rather than a real thing, and so cannot be the object of natural desire. Natural man does not calculate, whereas the actions which Rousseau pillories in his enemies are precisely the fruit of calculation. It is for this reason that he presents so many of his misdeeds (including the infamous accusation of Marion in Book 2) as the result of sudden impulse. Being a natural man in society, he has behaved impetuously and foolishly rather than schemingly or wickedly.

Two further features of the hero's character are worth

mentioning in this connection: the difficulty he has in writing and his laziness. Writing is associated with the more advanced and corrupt forms of society. When therefore Rousseau explains in Book 3 (I, 113) how 'this slowness of thought joined to this liveliness of feeling' made writing a torment for him, we should understand that he is closer to nature than those who write more easily. The paradox is that he was a successful writer, his best social strategy being 'to conceal myself and write', but as we shall shortly see, Jean-Jacques is not just a natural man. His 'incredible laziness', finally, connects easily with the images of primitive humanity in the *Discourse on Inequaliy*. When, having seen the failure of his first ambitions in Paris, he 'abandoned [himself] calmly to [his] idleness and to the care of Providence' (I, 287), he was acting like the improvident Caribs, who are supposed to sell their bedding in the morning and have nothing to sleep on in the evening.

Rousseau thus composes a picture of a simple, impetuous, unreflecting person who is out of his element in Paris society. The portrait serves to defend his character against attacks, but it is also an empirical verification of the ideas found in the *Discourse* and *Emile*. And because we all originate in natural man, it can claim general relevance; it is, as he suggests, a 'point of comparison', and it may provide a useful example. At the same time Jean-Jacques is an exception. The opening page declares: 'I am not made like anyone I have seen; I am bold enough to believe that I am not made like anyone who exists.' Perhaps, as his critics suggested, this proclamation of singularity was a sign of vanity, a bid for attention; it is certainly a recurrent theme of the auto-biography, so much so that if Rousseau is really as exceptional as he suggests, this might seem to undermine the usefulness of his work as a contribution to human psychology.

If he is unique, it may be because, by some quirk of fate, he is the only person to have retained in modern society the universal features of natural man − 'a man in all the truth of nature'. In this he would resemble the imaginary hero of

Emile, who seems a prodigy precisely because he alone has been brought up according to nature. This is not the whole story, however; Rousseau insists too much on the incomprehensible strangeness of his character and behaviour for them to be understood simply as a peculiar survival of nature within society.

Contradictions

At several points in his autobiography, he sums up his strangely contradictory nature. These summaries vary in emphasis, but always there is a stress on the combination of apparent opposites. Near the beginning of Book 1, we read of 'this heart at once so proud and so tender, this character at the same time effeminate and indomitable' (I, 12). Later in the same book, the emphasis is more on the ups and downs in his nature: 'I have ardent passions, and while they stir me nothing can equal my impetuosity', but 'all of that lasts only a moment, and the moment which follows casts me into a state of annihilation. Catch me in such periods of calm and you will find me the soul of indolence and timidity' (I, 36). This idea is used extensively in Part II to explain the inconsistencies of his behaviour. In particular, the important recapitulation of his career and character in Book 9 explains how after giving himself over to his intrepid passion for virtue during his heroic period, he sank back into his natural timidity on returning to the countryside. But this did not mean a return to a state of equilibrium:

If this revolution had merely restored me to myself and stopped there, all would have been well; but unfortunately it went further and carried me rapidly to the other extreme. Since that time my fluctuating soul has done nothing but pass to and fro across the line of repose, and its constantly renewed oscillations have never allowed it to remain there.   (I, 417)

This suggests perhaps the idea of a basic, original nature (calm, timid, indolent), but if so, this nature is one that cannot be recovered in the circumstances in which Rousseau finds himself.

Similar descriptions occur elsewhere, and from all of them emerges the image of a character pulled in different directions by contradictory impulses. Often it goes even further: 'there are times when I am so unlike myself that you would take me for someone with a character opposite to mine' (I, 128). The very notion of a fundamental nature is placed in some doubt here. Rousseau is estranged from Jean-Jacques, like an actor from some character he finds himself playing. In the grip of some 'folly' or 'delirium', the hero does strange things that seem to the narrator to defy explanation. The word most often used for such behaviour is 'bizarre', and there are many examples of 'bizarrerie' in the *Confessions*, some fairly trivial, such as the departure from Turin with Bâcle (Book 3) or the concert at Lausanne (Book 4), others, such as the accusation of Marion (Book 2), heavy with incalculable consequences. The most interesting case is provided by Jean-Jacques's behaviour after the illumination of Vincennes, the period of 'intoxication' or 'effervescence' lasting four or five years in which he becomes a new man: 'I was truly transformed; my friends and acquaintances could no longer recognise me' (I, 416–17). It was this period that made him a famous writer and a European celebrity. At the time when he was writing the *Confessions*, Rousseau viewed this as a disastrous development, the source of all his miseries. Presenting it, like the more comic 'bizarreries' of Book 4, as a deviation from his true nature, he attempts again to preserve his fundamental idea of himself as the loving, innocent, timid person whom we see in Book 1, the Charmettes episode and elsewhere.

Nevertheless, the natural man of the *Discourse on Inequality* was not subject to such moments of alienation. Jean-Jacques's impetuous passions are less culpable than the cool scheming of his enemies, certainly, but they too were supposedly unknown to our indolent forebears. He is not 'natural man', any more than the child of the *Confessions* is the reconstruction of the natural boy one sees in *Emile*. Something has to be explained, and the explanation takes us into the story of Rousseau's development.

Nature or nurture? This was one of the key questions for eighteenth-century philosophers as they tried to establish a new science of man. Rousseau hesitates. In Book 1, exploring the sources of his adult dispositions, he writes: 'thus did this heart, at once so proud and so tender, begin to be formed or to be revealed in me' (I, 12) — in other words these impulses may be inborn, a part of his inheritance. Similarly, attributing his hate of injustice to his unfair punishment at Bossey, he comments: 'This may be natural to me and I think it is' (I, 20); in this case experience reinforces a natural inclination. And most significantly of all, at the very beginning, he speaks of his one legacy from his parents: a 'sensitive heart', which 'produced all the misfortunes of my life' (I, 7).

There is then the strong suggestion that some of his emotional attitudes are innate, even if he cannot trace their origins — like the 'other cause, more secret and more powerful' that attaches him to Lake Geneva and that remains unexplained (I, 152). But since the *Confessions* tell of a man's experience of the world, the emphasis naturally falls on the influence exerted by the environment, and particularly by other people — parents, masters, friends, fellow citizens, benefactors, enemies. His experience is social, and he writes to show how society shapes the natural human being, for good and for bad.

Friendship, love, imagination

Sociability was not seen as an essential human quality in the *Discourse*, but by the time he came to write *Emile* Rousseau was describing humanity as 'naturally sociable, or at least destined to become so' (IV, 600). The social grouping nearest to nature is the family, and it is here that we see Jean-Jacques developing his loving disposition: 'to be loved by all who came near me was my dearest wish' (I, 14). It is clear from the passage from Book 1 analysed in the last chapter that in the family circle the boy is an example of the proper development of natural instincts in an environment governed by affection rather than power. In Rousseau's terms, natural love of self and pity can combine in such circumstances to produce the sociable emotions. The work of the family is then continued in friendship, first of all with the inseparable cousin Bernard, who is both relative and friend. Thereafter, throughout the *Confessions*, we are to be reminded of the author's capacity for friendship, usually (on the classical model) with men. Such relationships as that with the Spanish diplomat Altuna are offered as examples of true friendship, which in his eyes calls for complete openness, trust, reciprocity and equality. Not suprisingly, measuring reality against such standards, he was often disappointed in adult life. Apparent friends betray his trust (like Gauffecourt, or more seriously, Madame d'Epinay), attempt to dominate him (like Diderot) or fail to offer anything in return for his affection (like Grimm). And if friendship fails, this must be understood as the result of social pressures which isolate individuals from the loving community embodied in family life and glimpsed in such societies as old-world Geneva.

Family affection and friendship are both highly desirable products of social life. This is not so true of another development, the growth of the imagination. Here indeed, the *Confessions* echo the many novels from *Don Quixote* onwards which have warned against the perils of fiction. Encouraged by his father, the six-year-old boy discovers books, first of all novels (the long romantic novels of the French seventeenth century) and then more 'serious' literature, foremost among which are the *Lives* of Plutarch, inspiring biographies of the heroes of classical antiquity. In their different ways, both of these open up for the innocent reader horizons of perfection which transform him – and contribute greatly to the contradictions of his character. Plutarch figures in the *Confessions*, alongside Rousseau's father and Geneva, as the source of his 'free and republican spirit', his 'indomitable and proud character, impatient of servitude and the yoke, which has tormented me all my life in the situations least suited to allow it to develop freely' (I, 9). The child becomes the hero of his reading, a Greek or

Roman citizen adrift in the modern world. The seed sown here will flourish above all in Books 8 and 9 when the success of the first discourse 'finally brought to a head the first ferment of heroism and virtue which had been put there in my childhood by my father, my country and Plutarch' (I, 356). It is this which leads him, in his behaviour, his writings and his personal reform, to adopt a role 'so contrary to my nature'. His attitude to this period of 'intoxication' is very mixed; he is very proud of his work, but sees it as his personal downfall.

Plutarch generates imaginary or real heroism; novels do the same for love. Here Rousseau is more severe; he writes that this 'dangerous method', in which reading comes before experience, 'gave me bizarre and romantic notions of human life of which experience and reflexion have never really been able to cure me' (I, 8). So we see him at the Hermitage playing the 'extravagant shepherd', the hero of a comic novel, who sees the world through the distorting lens of fiction. His affair with Madame d'Houdetot is the outcome of his romantic imagination: 'She came, I saw her, I was drunk with love without an object, this intoxication fascinated my eyes, the object became fixed on her, I saw my Julie in Madame d'Houdetot, and soon I saw only Madame d'Houdetot, but decked out in all the perfections with which I had adorned the idol of my heart' (I, 440). This does not mean that his love was unreal, but this violent phsyical passion has its origins partly in the tendency of the young Jean-Jacques to people his imagination with 'beings after my own heart'. Novels provide the first model; the recourse to fantasy springs from frustration in the real world. It is towards the end of Book 1, when the hero is morally crippled by the domination of a bad master, that he finds an alternative life in the world of his imagination. He shows how this 'love of imaginary objects', filling the void in the heart of an affectionate person, gives him a taste for solitude (the solitude which is also, paradoxically, the state of original, unimaginative humanity). Thereafter in the *Confessions*, whenever he is alone or dissatisfied with the world around him, we see him building himself an alternative world. There is a strong erotic element in such fantasising; in Book 3 it is specifically linked with the 'disastrous' habit of masturbation. It also has a darker side: the person who can invent paradises after his own heart is prone to imagine threats and dangers – a lucid passage in Book 11 (I, 556) shows how his mind constructs a horror novel on the basis of a few obscure details.

One further example of his behaviour in love will show how important he thought this aspect of life for an understanding of his character. This is the encounter in Book 7 with the Venetian courtesan Zulietta, which he introduces with the promise, 'if there is one circumstance in my life which gives a good idea of my nature, it is the one I am about to relate' (I, 320). In the tragicomic story that follows, he fails to take advantage of the charming willingness of a ravishing young woman, and again it seems to be imagination that is to blame. She is so perfect, he thinks, that there must be something wrong with her, and his fevered mind manages to transform her into a kind of monster, with the result that he cannot play his manly part and is covered with shame. What is the cause of this behaviour? Rousseau does not give a fundamental explanation. He shows the bizarre workings of his imagination and mocks his own 'extravagance'. A reader might wish to invoke his family history, his relations with his aunt of Madame de Warens, but he simply (and question-beggingly) ascribes the whole thing to 'nature': 'Nature did not make me to know sexual pleasure. She put into my foolish head the wherewithal to poison this inexpressible happiness, the desire for which she placed in my heart.'

His masochistic tendencies also remain something of a mystery to him. True, he explains them as the result of being spanked by Mademoiselle Lambercier, whom he loved as a mother 'or perhaps more'; this 'decided my tastes, my desires, my passions, my being, for the rest of my life' (I, 41). But in fact the problem is more complicated. He himself points to the importance of his unusually 'chaste' upbringing, his 'natural timidity', and his 'romantic outlook'. Beyond this he does not venture, but the question poses itself as it does with Zulietta: is such behaviour 'in nature'? In terms of the *Discourse on Inequality*, the answer is 'no'. In that work sexual life is uncomplicated, desire is easily satisfied, passion is unknown. In the *Confessions*, on the other hand, Rousseau shows a man at least as far removed from such a primitive sort of nature as most of his readers; he ventures a number of possible explanations, but in the end he remains puzzled by this central aspect of existence. Nor, incidentally, does he present his deviation from nature as simply decadence. As with his Roman heroism, he shows the benefits such strange behaviour can bring. Thus his submissive behaviour with Madame Basile may not be natural, but 'in all my life I have not known a sweeter moment' (I, 76).

Degeneration

Friendship, affection, love, heroism, imagination – as these evolve in social life they produce some of the contradictions noted earlier, but they are all potentially valuable acquisitions. The history of mankind in the *Discourse on Inequality* is however above all one in which the species degenerates as social relations deteriorate. This pessimistic scheme is reflected in the *Confessions*, where Rousseau shows how the influences of a badly ordered society can corrupt individuals. The narrator-hero is the only character for whom this process of degeneration is shown in any detail, but it can be applied to many of the hundreds of people who cross the stage, from the Maréchal de Luxembourg, who is made cautious by court life, to the peasant, whose mean behaviour is explained by the iniquitous taxation system. Apart from Jean-Jacques, the one person whose inner life is explored is Madame de Warens. Her path of exile and apostasy resembles that of her protégé, and one can easily see how his explanations of her conduct in Books 2 and 3 place the blame for her faults on the society in which she grew up. For of course one of the functions of this way of presenting events is to shift the blame from the individual to the environment.

As far as Jean-Jacques is concerned, the degeneration

begins as Bossey with the discovery of masochism and the unjust punishment for the broken comb (these two incidents being connected in a way that has been interestingly investigated by Philippe Lejeune in *Le Pacte autobiographique*). Once power relations have replaced mutual confidence, 'we were less ashamed of doing wrong, and more frightened of being accused; we began to conceal our doings, to rebel, to lie' (I, 21). This is only a foretaste of the much worse fall from grace that occurs when the hero is separated from his cousin Bernard and sent out as an apprentice, first with a lawyer, then with the engraver Ducommun. It is the latter who is given the real villain's part, not so much for any personal vices (though he is 'crude and violent') as for the tyranny he exercises. The child experiences an abrupt transition 'from filial dependence to servile slavery' (I, 31). As Rousseau tells the tale, this results in the rapid transformation of an innocent and charming child into a liar and a thief with low tastes. He observes that 'in spite of the most honest education, I must have had a great tendency to degenerate'. In this the child's path is like that of natural man, whose goodness, unlike the virtue that depends on reason and experience, is extremely vulnerable. It is for this reason that the 'natural education' of *Emile* begins by setting up a strong fence to protect the tender plant.

After his initial decline and fall, Jean-Jacques is subjected to all manner of influences. Although there are many good individuals who try to help him towards virtue and happiness, social institutions, from the Hospice of Turin to the Parlement of Paris, are mostly seen as forces for evil. In Book 9 Rousseau tells us how he had realised 'that everything depended essentially on politics, and that however one set about it, no people would ever be anything but what the nature of its government made it' (I, 404). This remark concerns peoples rather than individuals, it is true, but even in the private *Confessions* politics has an important part. Although there is little discussion of constitutional matters as such, the whole book is informed by a vision of badly ordered societies in which inequality prevails.

This is visible almost from the beginning. When Jean-Jacques is sent to board at Bossey, he is treated differently from his cousin, who is of a slightly superior social rank. This difference, almost unnoticeable in childhood, is exacerbated as the boys reach adolescence: 'He was a boy of the upper town. I was a wretched apprentice, a mere child of Saint Gervais [a popular quarter of Geneva]. In spite of our birth there was no equality between us any more; he would have been letting himself down by frequenting me' (I, 42). From this time on, the poor hero has to suffer the caprices of masters and patrons and the humiliation of poverty and dependence. He will become a proud republican and a fierce opponent of injustice. Several incidents are described which contribute to this passion. The scene with the peasant in Book 4 sows 'the seed of that unquenchable hate which developed subsequently in my heart against all the vexations suffered by the unfortunate common people, and against their oppressors' (I, 164). Then, some fifteen years later, his unfortunate experiences with the ambassador in Venice 'left in my soul a seed of indignation against our stupid civil institutions, where the true common good and real justice are always sacrificed to some apparent order, which is in fact destructive of all order and simply adds the sanction of public authority to the oppression of the weak and the iniquity of the strong' (I, 327). This is the voice that was heard in the *Discourse on Inequality*.

Naturally, therefore, Rousseau tends to tell his story so as to contrast the great unfavourably with the humble. This shows for instance in his treatment of beneficence. Throughout his years of wandering, the hero receives help from a variety of modest individuals, such as the innkeeper at Lausanne whose 'simple and unshowy humanity' is set against the larger but more ostentatious (and often less useful) favours received from wealthier patrons (I, 146–7). It is against the privileged classes that he deliberately defines himself in his personal reform and his decision to earn his living by copying music rather than depend on a sinecure from a tax-farmer. From 1750 onwards he identifies as far as possible with the common people; it is this refusal of privilege that gives him his justification − in theory at least − for preferring to have his children brought up in the Foundlings' Home to become honest workers.

Not all of Rousseau's powerful benefactors are treated harshly, however. Not to speak of Madame de Warens, who is in a different category altogether, he paints highly sympathetic portraits of the Maréchal de Luxembourg and Earl Marischal Keith. With these two men at least he shows himself enjoying a genuinely equal friendship that transcends the divisions of rank. But even here there are difficulties. How can the 'friend of equality' decently spend his time at the Château de Montmorency? How can he find the right tone for talking to his social superiors, neither flattering nor uncouth? (His refusal of a gift of game from the Prince de Conti he describes as 'less the delicacy of a proud man . . . than the uncouth behaviour of an uneducated one' (I, 543).) However tactful the great may be, the very existence of such inequality is potentially a corrupting force.

Does Rousseau then represent himself as actually corrupted by society rather than simply suffering from its injustices? We have seen how the apprenticeship to Ducommun turned him into a liar and a thief. His later experiences, once he has left Geneva, will also make him vain and ambitious. The *Discourse on Inequality* told how social man, rather than living in and for himself, learns to live in the eyes of others. Rousseau says in Book 1 that he was by nature as free of vanity as anyone who has ever lived, but later on we come to see a man extraordinarily obsessed with the appearance he makes. An important notion here is that of shame. It is this, Rousseau says, that made him falsely accuse the servant girl Marion of stealing a ribbon in Turin: 'invincible shame conquered everything . . . shame alone was the cause of my impudence' (I, 86). In a more comic vein, it is shame that makes him blurt out silly things in conversation, particularly in the demanding world of the Paris salons, and keeps him constantly in fear that those around him may be mocking him.

The more positive component of vanity is the desire for distinction. Much of the *Confessions* can be read as the story, told with the bitter wisdom of age, of a young man's foolish ambitions. In an unequal society the imaginative Jean-Jacques, devourer of novels, naturally aspires to glamorous heights. He dreams in Turin of conquering a princess; as he walks to Paris he weaves fantasies of his future as a marshal in the French army. Such aspirations are treated with indulgent humour, unlike the more serious ambitions of his enemies Wintzenried and Grimm. It does not appear that Jean-Jacques is really corrupted, more that he allows himself to be momentarily dazzled by 'great expectations' (the expression is used several times in Book 2) and overlooks the possibilities of modest happiness offered by a working life in Geneva or marriage with Mademoiselle Merceret in Fribourg (Book 4, p. 145). At the beginning of Book 9, looking back over his Parisian years of worldly success, Rousseau declares that 'in the whirlpool of high society', enveloped in the 'incense of fame', he had never ceased to long for 'blessed rural leisure' (I, 401). In the next book he enumerates (with every appearance of satisfaction) the high nobility whom he received at Montlouis, but appeals to those who knew him at this time to say 'if they ever noticed that this glamour dazzled me for a moment, or if the vapour of this incense went to my head' (I, 527).

It may be that, as he suggests here, he did in fact preserve his original, natural simplicity through all the changes of his life. The story of this life is one of dramatic transformation, however, and not just a story of degeneration and loss, but one of success and achievement. The cards are stacked against the poor outsider, but he conquers his rightful place thanks to his merit and his passionate devotion to truth. This notion of one's 'place' figures prominently at several points in the *Confessions*. One of the most interesting is that of the dinner at Turin in Book 3, excellently analysed by Jean Starobinski in his *La Relation critique*. The young Jean-Jacques is serving at table; this is his place in the arbitrary hierarchy of society. Then suddenly (prefiguring Julien Sorel in Stendhal's *The*

Scarlet and the Black) he attracts the attention of the company – and of the young lady of the household – with his unexpected erudition: 'it was one of those too rare moments which replace things in their natural order and avenge humiliated merit on the outrages of fortune' (I, 96). So later in Venice he wins the respect of all by his firm and virtuous conduct and temporarily reverses his subordination to the unworthy ambassador; so too at Fontainebleau, on the opening night of his opera, he becomes the object of general admiration and triumphs over the malicious hostility of the musical establishment.

In the latter case, as in the dinner at Turin, there is a strong erotic element in his triumph, as Rousseau himself notes:

> I am . . . sure that at this moment it was more a question of sexual gratification than of authorial vanity, and certainly if there had been only men there, I should not have been constantly consumed, as I was, with the desire to drink with my lips the delicious tears I had caused to flow. (I, 378)

In spite of the murky depths and humiliations that he explores, his autobiography is at least superficially a story of success in love. Not a story of numerous conquests, to be sure, for we are told repeatedly that Jean-Jacques's timidity and peculiar tastes prevent him from playing the part of a Casanova. Often we see him ridiculously falling in love with the first woman he meets. On the other hand, he shows himself repeatedly as the object of women's affection or desire, so much so that he apologises: 'I am sorry to be making so many girls fall in love with me' (I, 144). The high point of such favour is perhaps the brief encounter with Madame de Larnage (Book 6), where through the comic tone the reader can sense Rousseau's satisfaction in recounting his success: 'Never have my eyes, my senses and my heart spoken so eloquently . . .' (I, 252).

Paradise lost

This adventure is, however, the prelude to one of the disastrous turning points in the book, the loss of 'Maman': the success story is more than counter-balanced by the tragedy of paradise lost. Paradise is the place of happiness, and the exploration of this notion is one of the main concerns of the *Confessions*. Here again, as in his analysis of his own nature, Rousseau presents the reader with one particular case, but by associating his personal idea of happiness with the idea of nature, he offers a model with which readers can associate themselves. This 'discourse of happiness' has in fact been one of the main attractions of the book to generations of readers.

Of the different visions of happiness presented to us, some of the most memorable are those which involve a moment of awakening. Here, for instance, in very simple terms, is the hero waking up after an idyllic night in the open air by the river at Lyon: 'My sleep was sweet, my awakening was still sweeter. It was broad daylight; my eyes as they opened saw water, greenery, an admirable landscape' (I, 169). In Les Charmettes he is up before the sun and walks through an orchard and up the hill (I, 236); in the Hermitage he wakes after a short sleep to hear the nightingale and exclaims: 'All my wishes have come true' (I, 403). Both of these last two periods, as Rousseau's imagination work on them, acquire similar characteristics. Above all, there is the simplicity of country life, taking one back to the town boy's first acquaintance with the country in the earlier paradise of Bossey. Stripped of care and self-love, the waking individual is in harmony through his senses with the basic elements of life: greenery, air and above all, water. 'I have always loved water passionately', writes Rousseau in his evocation of the Island of Saint-Pierre (I, 642), which was to be the subject of the beautiful fifth 'walk' of the *Reveries of the Solitary Walker*. In this later work he tries to analyse the happiness given by such a simple, solitary, passive existence. The essential point is the idea of permanence or continuity. The pleasures of the world (as he often calls them) may be intense, but they are too infrequent or short-lived to constitute a state of happiness; happiness is rather 'a simple and lasting state, which has nothing vivid in itself, but whose permanence increases its charm to such an extent that we find in it at last supreme happiness' (I, 1046). At such times one enjoys 'nothing external to oneself, nothing but oneself and one's own existence'.

In 'The Garden', Andrew Marvell writes mockingly:

Two paradises 'twere in one
To live in paradise alone.

Rousseau's paradise does often seem a solitary one, like the state of his natural man. Some of the most striking passages in the *Confessions* show us the young man walking, free as air, free to contemplate and dream. Take for instance the marvellous pages at the end of Book 4 where he is walking from Lyon to Chambéry, stopping to gaze at the mountain torrents and the birds of prey, rolling stones down the mountain side: 'I delighted to see them rolling, leaping, shattering into a thousand pieces before they reached the bottom of the precipice' (I, 173). Or again, some forty years later, his feelings as he drifts out on the lake of Bienne, alone in a boat: 'The moment when I drifted away gave me a joy which even made me tremble, a joy I cannot express, and whose cause I cannot truly understand' (I, 643). There is an important difference here: in the first case, the hero knows that he is on his way back to the affections of 'Maman'; in the second, on the other hand, he is a persecuted man, and Rousseau goes on to suggest that the cause of his pleasure was perhaps 'a secret satisfaction of being . . . out of reach of the wicked'. In other words, there is a continuing ability to find happiness in solitude, but this becomes for the harassed author of Part II a consolation for the misfortunes of his life rather than a complement to a happy social life. As he repeatedly says, he is naturally a loving person; his apparent misanthropy is a result of his sufferings. Often when he speaks of a happy solitude, it turns out to be a shared isolation. The true human paradise is a community.

This happy state corresponds in a way to the 'golden age' of the *Discourse on Inequality*, the beginnings of society when the benefits of living together have not yet been out-weighed by the disadvantages. One of the essential requirements of this life is that it be lived in a relatively small enclosed world − like the idyllic community at Clarens which Rousseau dreams up for the heroes of *La Nouvelle Héloïse*. Just as the infant Jean-Jacques is protected from the rough streets by the family circle, so at Les Charmettes, the Hermitage or the Island of Saint-Pierre he is separate and secure. (The island on the lake is the ideal image for this situation.) Like the garden in Voltaire's *Candide*, this enclosed world is not a place of idleness, not even the Island of Saint-Pierre, where Jean-Jacques takes part in the apple harvest. In the Hermitage and Les Charmettes, too, he and those around him engage in simple rustic tasks. The calm and well-being he values so much come precisely from a steady and undemanding routine. Rousseau is one of the great singers of the pleasures of ordinary life − pleasures accessible to all, as opposed to the heady joys of vanity, which he associates with the sophisticated life of the city.

In all these cases happiness is connected with country life and the natural world, but Rousseau was a town boy and he did of course have a vision of civic happiness in a well-ordered city. This is not very apparent in the *Confessions*, which are the work of his more solitary old age. There is however the brief passage at the end of Book 1 on the contented life of the modest citizen, and there is also an interesting urban parallel to the periods of rural contentment in the episode of the Annecy singing school in Book 3 (I, 122−3). This is not a time of ecstacy, but 'one of those I have spent in the greatest tranquillity and that I have had the greatest pleasure in remembering'. Here Jean-Jacques is part of an enclosed yet active community which gives him a humble part to play, just enough to satisfy his innocent 'pride' as he plays a recorder solo or sings a duet. The life here revolves round music, which is almost always associated with happiness for Rousseau − one recalls the deep emotions generated in Book 1 by the memory of Aunt Suzanne's singing, or the 'sweet harmony' and 'angelic chants' of the Italian opera which wake him in Book 7 to the feeling that he is 'in Paradise' (I, 314). Music, flowing like water, establishes profound connections between one person and another, between past and present.

Other features of the singing-school episode are worth noting. To start with, there are 'the surrounding objects, the temperature of the air, its smell, its colour, a certain local impression which was felt only there, and whose vivid memory transports me there afresh'. For Rousseau, pleasure attaches itself to the perception and memory of everyday objects, and sense perceptions, including smell and touch, play a vital play in the recovery of lost time – the periwinkle in Book 6 of the *Confessions* anticipates the 'petite madeleine' in Proust's *A la recherche du temps perdu*. Then there is the 'good dinner that awaited us' and 'the good appetite we brought to it'. One of the principal ingredients of happiness for the simple man Rousseau wants to be is the consumption of good unpretentious meals in good company and with a good appetite. A beautiful example of this is the brief passage in Book 8, where we see the hero and Thérèse sitting at their fourth-floor window overlooking Paris and eating a simple supper of bread, cheese, cherries and wine, seasoned with 'friendship, trust, intimacy, tenderness of soul' (I, 354).

It is these final ingredients above all that bring happiness. They are sometimes associated with Thérèse, particularly in the early years of their relationship, and it is worth emphasising the part played by this much maligned and loyal woman in providing Rousseau with the support he needed to write and to endure misfortune during his last thirty years. In the *Confessions*, however, he is concerned with the past, and he dwells less on his current companion than on the woman he had lost, Madame de Warens. Jean-Jacques's love for 'Maman' is not the passion that shakes him in the presence of Madame d'Houdetot; it is an innocent affection, a 'perfect trust', which gives him 'peace of mind, calm, serenity, security, confidence' (I, 52). Rousseau himself indicates how close this is to the relation between mother and child, and we may see in her the reincarnation of the lost mother, or more plausibly of the loving Aunt Suzanne who sang to the little boy in the enclosed family home in Geneva. When this loving relationship is situated in the rural setting of Les Charmettes, the ideal conditions for happiness are present; when the loving trust collapses, the paradise vanishes.

All of these happpy states are guiltless, guilt being associated in particular with sexuality. Rousseau may find satisfaction in telling of his affair with Madame de Larnage, and he makes no secret of his relations with 'Maman' and Thérèse or of his desire for Madame d'Houdetot, but the times of true happiness seem to be those in which sexual desire is either absent or sublimated. At such times he can play a part like that of the innocent child. Even at Les Charmettes, where he was Madame de Waren's lover, he minimises this aspect of the situation: 'I went to kiss her in bed; she was often half asleep, and this kiss, as pure as it was tender, took from its very innocence a charm which has never accompanied the pleasure of the senses' (I, 237). Such episodes as the scene with Madame Basile (Book 2) or the outing to Toune with the two young ladies (Book 4) show Jean-Jacques in a state of passive innocence, which he claims to prefer to intenser pleasures. This is the appeal of the triangular situation in which the inoffensive affection of friendship dominates the disturbing force of love. Rousseau presents himself as happy between the two girls at Toune and happy to share Madame de Warens with Claude Anet, and he imagines an ideal dénouement to his love for Madame d'Houdetot in which he would be the innocent participant in the mutual love of Sophie and Saint Lambert.

This last example is an imaginary solution to an unhappy situation, and it is a variation on the happy scenario dreamed up by Rousseau in *La Nouvelle Héloïse*, where the errant hero Saint Preux is brought into the loving community of Clarens, no longer as lover but as friend. For of course happiness is found in the imagination as much as in reality. As well as the descriptions of the composition of the novel in Book 9, the *Confessions* contain many evocations of the enchanted world of fiction in which 'I am master of the whole of nature; my heart wanders from object to object, uniting and identifying itself with those that please it, surrounding itself with charming images, intoxicating itself on delicious feelings' (I,

162). This may be only a second best, a consolation in an imperfect world, but there are times when it seems to be enough, or even better than reality. Describing himself walking back to the assured happiness of his reunion with Madame de Warens, Rousseau notes: 'My ideas were peaceful and gentle, not heavenly and exhilarating' (I, 178). There is a conflict here between ecstacy and contentment. Having lived in the innocent paradise of Clarens, his heroine Julie dies unsatisfied and writes in a religious profession of faith before she dies: 'In this world the land of the imagination is the only one worth living in' (II, 693). In spite of all we have seen in the last few pages, there is in Rousseau an idealism that reality can never truly satisfy. The essence of paradise is that it is lost. If therefore we are looking for the source of happiness in the *Confessions*, we may find it not so much in the actual situations described (Bossey, Les Charmettes) as in the activities of memory and imagination which recreate or create them.

Virtue

Whatever the possibilities of retaining the child's ability to be happy or recovering former happiness in memory, the *Confessions* tell a story of loss. This loss may however bring with it a compensatory gain. In earlier works Rousseau had described how humanity loses its original happiness and innocence, but acquires new qualities in the process. Natural man was merely good; social man has the possibility of becoming virtuous, of exercising his reason and will to control his passions. Something of this is present in the *Confessions*, if not as a major theme, then at least as a recurring refrain from Book 6 onwards. This is how the narrator, using yet again the metaphor of germination, presents his state after he has lost his place in 'Maman' 's affections: 'Thus with my misfortunes the virtues began to germinate which had their seeds deep in my soul, which my studies had cultivated, and which only needed the ferment of adversity to bring them into flower' (I, 264). What comes to the fore now is the idea of sacrifice, which is linked, as we shall see shortly, with that of expiation. Jean-Jacques sacrifices his own interest to that of 'Maman'; later, in Books 9 and 11, we see him preferring the peace of mind of Madame d'Houdetot and Madame de Luxembourg to his own reputation. More generally, in Part II, the erring but basically innocent boy of the early books becomes first the intrepid champion of freedom and justice, and then a willing martyr for the truth. Here he approaches an even more exalted role, that of Socrates or Christ. So he writes of his feelings just before his condemnation by the Paris Parlement: 'I waited quietly for the outcome, relying on my integrity and my innocence in the whole affair, and only too happy, whatever persecution lay in store for me, to be called to the honour of suffering for the truth' (I, 579).

A related aspect of the hero's moral progress is stoical resignation. Quite early on in Book 5, illness teaches him to detach himself from his fate, accepting whatever comes to him from the hands of Providence and devoting himself to his real duties – so much so that Rousseau can declare: 'I can truly say that I only began to live when I came to regard myself as a dead man' (I, 228). Paradoxically perhaps, adversity brings him back to the calm acceptance which he attributes to natural man, so that even if he is expelled from paradise he can find happiness in himself. Here we return to the theme of solitude, which is at once natural and unnatural: when he is separated physically from his adversaries, Rousseau can once again content himself with his own existence and the world of his imagination. If the *Confessions* were to provide moral examples to readers, then for the Rousseau of the 1760s this was one of the most important of them. At the end of Book 11 he contrasts 'all the great philosophers who are so superior to the adversity they have never experienced' (I, 587) with the persecuted Jean-Jacques, fleeing from Paris alone in his post-chaise, but retaining in the storm the peace of mind needed to write the biblical prose poem, *The Levite of Ephraim*.

Destiny and guilt

Misfortune and loss may transform the protagonist of the *Confessions* into something like a tragic hero; the question remains, as in tragedy: Why should all this happen to him? Rousseau suggests a number of answers: society, a conspiracy, destiny, his own fault.

I have already discussed the way society is seen as disfiguring the young and innocent Jean-Jacques. Parisian manners are made responsible for his decision to deposit his children in the Foundlings' Home; society corrupts him, with disastrous results for his own happiness. Elsewhere it attacks him: he falls foul of the institutions that compose it, from the guards who shut him out of Geneva to the Parlement that drives him out of France. Or it may not be institutions that are to blame so much as individuals. Rousseau presents himself as shabbily treated by Wintzenried, whose coarse egoism puts an end to the idyll of Les Charmettes, and by the Ambassador Montaigu, who cuts short his promising diplomatic career. The real disaster occurs in Book 9, with the expulsion from the Hermitage; in this case the blame is placed squarely on the hero's false friends, the *philosophes*, Madame d'Epinay, Diderot and above all Grimm.

At this point Rousseau takes a crucial step. Rather than simply blaming his fate on the hostile acts of separate individuals, he knits them all into a great conspiracy against himself. This is almost entirely confined to Part II, for the good reason that it only crystallised in the author's mind after most of Part I was written. What is more, his views on the matter changed; only in 1768 did he begin to suspect − quite mistakenly, as far as we know − that the gap in his papers for a period in 1756–7 was connected with a plan to associate him with an attempt on the king's life, and it was not until early in 1770 that he decided that Diderot had been associated with Grimm in the management of the whole affair. Nor did he ever think that he had got to the bottom of it. At the end of Book 11 and the beginning of Book 12, he encourages his readers to read the whole story carefully like detectives looking for clues and helping to find a global explanation of the mystery. Not that he expects to be surprised: 'I know for certain what will be the final outcome of their research, but I lose my way in the dark and twisting underground path which will lead them there' (I, 590).

The general outlines of this fantastic construction are laid out in Book 10 (I, 492–4). The whole system is supposed to be the product of the envy and resentment of a few individuals, notably Grimm (for the reasons suggested in Book 9) and the powerful government minister Choiseul (out of pique at a piece of blundering flattery in the *Social Contract*). In the winter of 1769–70, Rousseau was convinced that it all fitted together, and that all sorts of apparently significant words and actions could be explained by it. He therefore became an expert in the interpreting of signs – signs resurrected by memory some ten years later. The strange thing is that in Book 11 he gives an account of the way his imagination tormented him with a vision of conspiracy in 1762: 'It is amazing what a host of facts and circumstances came into my mind to fit this folly and give it an air of verisimilitude, nay, to show me how obvious and proven it was' (I, 566). He never applies this insight to his beliefs of 1770.

The malice of men and women was not, however, a sufficient explanation. Rousseau was a religious believer; he had written to Voltaire to defend Providence against the latter's attack in his *Poem on the Lisbon Earthquake* of 1755. The *Confessions* therefore contain numerous suggestions of a supernatural force at work behind the merely human machinations. This is usually called 'destiny', 'fate' or 'my star', but in Book 5 for instance he wonders whether it is not 'Providence' which is calling him to 'great trials' (I, 205). Such language adds dramatic intensity to the narrative, as when Jean-Jacques finds himself shut out of Geneva: 'I shuddered as I saw these terrible horns lifted in the air, a sinister and fatal omen of the inevitable fate that this moment was inaugurating for me' (I, 42). The whole of the life-story is punctuated with such turning points. In Book 6 (I, 260) there is 'the fatal moment which was to bring in its wake the long chain of my misfortunes', but Book 8 too recounts 'the first origin of the long chain of my misfortunes' (I, 349). The notions of destiny and the chain of misfortunes give shape to the life; however oppressive they may seem, they offer some comfort to the victim, who can see himself as a being set apart, a sacred figure.

'The fault, dear Brutus, is not in our stars, / But in ourselves . . .': at one point only in the *Confessions* does the narrator cast doubt on the alibi of destiny. In the Hospice at Turin the Protestant Jean-Jacques is about to become a convert to Catholicism against his own conscience, 'and I groaned at the fate which had led me there, as if this fate had not been my own work' (I, 63). Are not the other misfortunes of his life also his 'own work'? Yes, but only up to a point. The book is a confession, after all, and he is willing to admit his guilt in several episodes, even if he suggests attenuating circumstances. But what is the connection between this guilt and his misfortunes? For Rousseau there is usually no direct link. If he has to leave the Hermitage the immediate cause is the malice of his enemies rather than his own behaviour; if he is condemned by the Paris Parlement, it is an act of arbitrary vindictiveness against his person rather than the predictable consequence of openly publishing unorthodox books in an intolerant society. The most important faults admitted in the *Confessions* are probably the accusation of Marion, the desertion of Le Maître in Lyon, the abandoning of 'Maman', the love for Madame d'Houdetot, and the placing of his children in a foundlings' home. The last two do indeed contribute something directly to Rousseau's misfortunes (exile, abuse), but the principal link between fault and suffering is to be sought rather in the religious notion of expiation of atonement. Of the abandoning of 'Maman', Rousseau writes: 'I thus deserved the most terrible punishments which have assailed me unceasingly since that time; may they atone for my ingratitude' (I, 392). On Marion he is even more explicit:

If it is a crime which can be atoned for, as I dare to hope it is, this must have been achieved by the many misfortunes which have assailed my last years, by forty years of integrity and honour in difficult circumstances, and poor Marion has found so many avengers in this world that however great my offence against her, I have little fear of taking my guilt with me'. (I, 87)

In the earlier Neuchâtel manuscript he had written simply: 'it must have been atoned for by the misfortunes of my life, which I have often endured patiently, regarding them as a just punishment'. The later version, probably written at the same time as Part II, not only introduces the author's forty years of virtue as a counterweight, but it transforms the makers of the conspiracy into unknowing instruments of divine justice. In so far as his crimes cannot be explained away as the unfortunate results of good intentions, they are purged away by suffering. Rousseau's innocence is restored for the Day of Judgement.

In chapter 1, I spoke of the different models proposed by Rousseau in such works as the *Discourse on Inequality* and *Emile*. In this chapter I have suggested how as he probes his past he simultaneously creates a comparable image of himself, how the good and simple child of nature develops in society, acquiring the contradictory characteristics that often give rise to incomprehensible behaviour, learning love and friendship and the power of the imagination, degenerating from his first innocence, but also, through the misfortunes inflicted on him by men and destiny, gaining new virtues of self-sacrifice and resignation, and atoning for the faults he had been led to commit. We have seen, too, through all these changes, the continuity of a nature which finds happiness in a simple, natural, loving existence. Rousseau has painted a character and a destiny which are both unique and exemplary. In telling his story he is describing and justifying himself, but also, as in the earlier works, proclaiming truths which he thinks humanity needs to hear, the lessons of natural goodness and happiness. I have tried here to draw out his own view of his life rather than to judge it. But in writing his *Confessions* he was presenting himself to his judges, the readers, and it is to their problems and reactions that we must now turn.

Chapter 5

The reader's problems

The implied reader

Who is the reader to whom the *Confessions* are directed? In reality, the work has been read by millions of people. Their reactions have been infinitely varied, and this chapter will refer to some of the most interesting of these. But how did Rousseau himself envisage his reader? One may gain a clue to this, as Huntington Williams suggests in his *Rousseau and Romantic Autobiography*, by looking at the scenes within the book where the hero tells his story to a listener. These listeners are sometimes people who played an important part in Rousseau's life, such as Madame de Warens, the Maréchale de Luxembourg and Malesherbes, but they may also be simply passing acquaintances. When in Book 4 the false Archimandrite is found out by the French ambassador at Soleure, Jean-Jacques as his secretary is also questioned and willingly tells all. The reaction is all that he could wish for:

He was so pleased with my little story and the heart-felt emotion with which he could see I had told it, that he took me by the hand, went to his wife's room and introduced me to her, giving her a summary of my tale. Madame de Bonac received me kindly.

(I, 156–7)

The sincere eloquence of the speaker convinces the listener, who enters sympathetically into his situation and transmits the story to a further listener. No one thinks to question the truth of the tale; a happy state of communion is created, something approaching the transparency of souls wished for by Rousseau.

Writing is not speaking; reading is not listening. As we read, far removed from the author, he cannot increase our conviction by the force of his presence. On the other hand,

Rousseau tells us in Book 3 that he actually prefers writing to speaking, since the writer, unlike the speaker, has time to prepare himself. As a writer he can hope to win over his reader in the first place by his obvious sincerity – the equivalent of the 'heart-felt emotion' which convinced the ambassador at Soleure. He believed that readers could distinguish between genuine and false emotion even in writing; he notes for instance that 'the letter to d'Alembert was full of a tenderness of soul which the public could feel to be genuine' (I, 502).

This natural persuasiveness is reinforced in the *Confessions* by continual appeals to the reader. Sometimes these are apologetic: Rousseau imagines a reluctant reader who needs to be persuaded to continue, if necessary by an appeal to his conscience. The introduction to Book 7 warns 'those who want to begin this book that as they read on, nothing can save them from boredom except the desire to complete their acquaintance with a man and the sincere love of justice and truth' (I, 279). Elsewhere the dialogue with the readers takes many different forms; the author takes us into his confidence, jokes with us, shares our astonishment; or else he may explain his way of proceeding, reassure us about his reliability and encourage us to take part in the process of discovery. Above all, as I showed in chapter 2, he puts his reader in the position of judge. In doing so, however, he is obviously not expecting a hostile judgement. For all that he may say at the end of Book 4 about readers' freedom to judge and interpret for themselves, he has a clearly defined view of his own character and destiny (outlined in the previous chapter), and he challenges us from the very outset to disagree with him. The fighting statement of the first page is echoed by the embarrassing declaration made at the end:

Whoever . . . examines for himself my nature, my character, my morals, my inclinations, my pleasures, my habits, and can think that I am a bad man, is himself a man who deserves to be put down [*étouffé*]. (I, 656)

This was said in the face-to-face situation of a public reading, where Rousseau wanted to force an acquittal. Like his first listeners, his readers are asked to accept his version of the truth, to take sides, for or against. It is this that makes reading the *Confessions* an uncomfortable experience, however warmly one may respond to the beautiful and entertaining scenes which abound in it.

Truth-telling

The most awkward question concerns truth. Rousseau's claim was to be a truth-teller; his chosen Latin motto means 'to devote óne's life to the truth'. It is not surprising then that his critics have devoted a good deal of energy to showing how his version of the facts diverges from what really happened. The first reaction of many early readers was to denounce episodes like the story of Madame de Warens's love life as slanderous misrepresentation. For over a hundred years the *Confessions* were treated primarily as a historical document, to be checked against other documents such as private letters or the 'pseudo-memoirs' of Madame d'Epinay (an autobiographical novel which she reworked with the help of Diderot and Grimm so as to give an alternative version of the Hermitage episode).

Now that some of the dust has settled, modern scholarship suggests that Rousseau's account of the external facts of his life is broadly correct, but inaccurate over details. Inaccuracy was no doubt inevitable in a work written largely from memory, and the author himself admits: 'I may leave things out, put them in the wrong order, make mistakes over dates' (I, 278). Thus we know, for instance, that he was about eleven (not eight) at the time of his chastisement at Bossey, that his conversion at Turin was quicker than he suggests, that he arrived in Paris in 1742 (not 1741), and that his stay at Les Charmettes with Madame de Warens was not so long or uninterrupted as it would appear from the *Confessions*. A good deal of research has been devoted to this last question in particular; on the strength of the date on a lease, some scholars have claimed that the idyll of Les Charmettes is all invented. It is generally accepted, however, that Rousseau's stay was a historical reality, even though in the 1760s he seems to have transferred to this site many of the feelings he had previously associated with the Hermitage. As his ideal crystallised round the earlier episode, he was led to present it as longer and less troubled than other evidence suggests. On such matters it is difficult for the modern historian to be absolutely sure; in the same way, there have been those who have asserted that he never had any children to deposit in the Foundlings' Home, but no real evidence supports this claim.

Reflecting on the problems of truth-telling in the fourth of his *Reveries*, Rousseau tells how in writing his memoirs he sometimes filled the gaps in memory with imaginary details or embellished the happy moments of his past with 'ornaments' (I, 1035). None of this, he says, was actually contrary to the truth. As he puts it in the preamble to the *Confessions*, 'I may have supposed as true what I knew to have been possible, but never what I knew to be false.' Presumably no reader would expect an autobiography, and particularly an account of the author's childhood, to be factually accurate in every detail. The problem is to draw the line between harmless ornament and significant alteration, whether intentional or not. When Rousseau makes himself three years younger than he really was at the time when Mademoiselle Lambercier spanked him, is this an insignificant detail, or would the replacement of an eight-year-old by an eleven-year-old not make the scene less innocent? And if the stay in the Turin hospice is shortened, this tends to make Jean-Jacques more of a heroic resister than he would otherwise have appeared.

These two examples look like minor changes in the author's favour. In the *Reveries* Rousseau admits that he did sometimes involuntarily present himself 'in profile' in the earlier work so as to hide his 'deformities', but he protests that 'these reticences were more than compensated for by other more bizarre omissions which often made me conceal the good more carefully than the bad' (I, 1036). Clearly (if one thinks of one's own memories) there have to be omissions in an autobiography; when Rousseau says that he must 'tell everything' or 'omit nothing' this means only that he must tell the bad as well as the good, and, as he says at the beginning of Book 7, 'make known my inner self in all the different situations of my life' (I, 278). Errors of detail, selection and omission must leave intact a true portrait. What is one to say of his truthfulness in this broad sense?

Particularly if one reads the *Confessions* in their historical setting, it is hard not to admire the boldness with which the author reveals some of the shameful episodes of his youth. The shocked and scornful reactions of many early readers give some idea of the revolutionary nature of his frankness in writing in all seriousness of such matters as his masochism, masturbation or tendency to petty larceny. 'An incredible tissue of puerility, folly and extravagance' wrote the journalist of the *Année littéraire* on the appearance of Part I – and until the twentieth century it was common to print the work in a censored form. Many of Rousseau's admirers regretted deeply that he had spoiled his image with such trivial and debasing confessions; this was to be the case some years later with George Sand, who suggested further, in the introduction to her *Story of my Life*, that he took a perverse pleasure in revealing his turpitude. On the other hand some readers (often younger ones) were much affected by his courage. The enlightened Ginguené wrote for instance in 1791: 'He had until then justified his motto [*Vitam impendere vero*] by telling mankind the truth about themselves; he justifies it in quite another way by telling them the truth about himself.'

Willingness to reveal one's shameful deeds or inclinations does not guarantee a true portrait, however. For some readers, indeed, this apparent frankness was a hypocritical tactic. In the article 'Memoirs' in his *Elements of Literature* (1787), Jean-François Marmontel, without naming his enemy Rousseau, clearly has him in mind when he writes of the 'ignoble trick' of accusing oneself 'either to make people say that one has dared to say what no one had previously dared to say, or to give credit, by a few humiliating confessions, to the praise one gives oneself by way of compensation'. Just as Rousseau accused Montaigne of mock modesty, so readers have seen *him* as managing in spite of his shocking revelations to give himself the innocent part – or even the part of hero. We saw in the last chapter how the *Confessions* presses on us the notion that Jean-Jacques is fundamentally good; it is not surprising if truth is sometimes a casualty in this vital struggle.

Distortion

There are many incidents where, without going beyond the author's text, one feels unable to adopt the conclusion he seems to be proposing. To take just one example, Book 6 contains the description of how Jean-Jacques decides not to resume his affair with Madame de Larnage. More than a page (I, 259–60) is devoted to his motives on this occasion; these include the remorse caused by his unfaithfulness to 'Maman', the strong likelihood that his English pseudonym, Dudding, would be exposed as the absurd lie it was, the awareness that 'my fancy had lost its first vivacity', the possibility that Madame de Larnage's family would be hostile, and the fear that he might fall in love with the daughter of the house. The last of these provokes the following eloquent reflections: 'Was I then to repay the mother's favours by attempting to corrupt her daughter, to set up the most shocking relationship, to bring dissension, dishonour, scandal and hell into the house?' The language is very strong, but hardly appropriate given what we know of his usual unenterprising behaviour when in love. It does however allow him to present his conduct as the outcome of heroic self-denial rather than timidity: 'I carried it out [his resolution not to resume the affair] with courage, and with a few sighs I admit; but also with the inner satisfaction I enjoyed for the first time in my life of saying to myself: I deserve my own esteem, for I am capable of prefering my duty to my pleasure.' The very style here suggests the straining to impose an acceptable face on a rather dubious episode.

All this one can get from the text itself. The difficulty is made worse when one discovers (from Rousseau's correspondence and other documents) that he already knew at this time that he had been supplanted in 'Maman''s affection by Wintzenried, of whom he speaks so vindictively in the following pages. In fact then, rather than going back to renew his former life (as the *Confessions* suggest) he was returning, after a disagreable stay in Montpellier, to a situation which he knew in advance to be degrading, but was presumably willing to endure in order to be with 'Maman' again and to regain some sort of security. None of this figures in the text, where he presents the discovery of the affair with Wintzenried *after* the return from Montpellier. One guesses that he does so, whether deliberately or by a significant lapse, in order to wipe away the memory of his own humiliation − and this in turn may give rise to the heroic presentation of his motives.

Rousseau claimed in the Neuchâtel preamble that only he could have direct access to what went on in his mind. One must indeed agree that although we may know more about his past than he tells us, we cannot really know his thoughts and feelings as he sat in his post-chaise on the way to Bourg St Andeol in 1738. On the other hand, even if our minds are not visible to others, we have learned to estimate the plausibility of people's descriptions of their feelings and motives in relation to what we know of their actions and situations. On such a reckoning it is very hard to believe what Rousseau writes about this episode. In this case indeed he touchingly provides enough information for the reader to draw conclusions different from his own − and one might argue that such inconsistencies in his account are in themselves a kind of veracity. A hostile critic, such as L. G. Crocker, will be more categorical, seeing this passage as 'a sheer fraud, part of the deliberate rearrangement of the facts that he carries out in the *Confessions* in order to shift the blame and discredit from himself to Madame de Warens' (*Jean-Jacques Rousseau*, I, 120).

In a similar way, most readers will be suspicious (and the more hostile will be contemptuous) of the superlatives, hyperboles or sharp oppositions of black and white which dot the work. Everything seems pushed to extremes, happiness or misery, goodness or badness. In places this concerns the lives of others (Grimm's strange malady in Book 8 for instance), but usually it underscores the uniqueness of the hero and his situation. Here are just a few examples among dozens: the six-year-old Jean-Jacques acquires 'a taste for literature which was rare and perhaps unique at that age' (I, 9); the friendship between him and his cousin is 'an example that is perhaps unique in the history of childhood' (I, 14); he returned from Italy 'as no one perhaps has ever returned at my age' (I, 108); the triangular relationship between himself, Madame de Warens and Claude Anet is 'a society perhaps without a parallel on earth' (I, 201). The 'perhaps' appears regularly as a concession to common sense, but Rousseau is driven again and again, unconsciously it seems (and often rather comically), to insist on his singularity and to present his enemies as the authors of a prodigious, unparalleled work of darkness. The obsessive use of such figures of speech as hyperbole, metaphor and antithesis suggests a constant distortion of reality.

Self-knowledge and memory

I do not believe that in presenting himself and his enemies in this unconvincing way Rousseau was acting hypocritically or deliberately telling lies. It is far more likely that he was deceiving himself − in the case of the conspiracy, to the point of madness. When he said truthfulness, he meant sincerity. He told the truth as he saw it, and was no doubt in good faith when he proclaimed in the *Reveries*, again with superlatives, that in the *Confessions* he had 'carried good faith, sincerity, truthfulness and frankness as far, further even − or so I believe − than has any other man' (I, 1035). Such confidence in the possibility of knowing and telling the truth about oneself appeared naive to the reasonable David Hume. When Rousseau argues that only we can know ourselves, the modern reader is likely to believe that it is just as difficult to know yourself as to know others. Nor is such scepticism particularly modern; the French moralist tradition, as represented by by Montaigne, Pascal or La Rochefoucauld, had insisted on the dark chasms of mind and heart, the infinite possibilities of self-deception, the occult machinations of self-love. Christian confessional literature is full of the same theme. Rousseau was familiar with such writing, but while directing his spotlight into many fascinating dark corners, he often seems blind to his own true nature.

In particular he underestimates the problems of memory. When he writes for instance, 'I cannot be mistaken about what I felt, nor about what my feelings made me do' (I, 278), the common pronoun 'I' masks the distance that exists between the present and the past self. Could he in 1767 really remember exactly what was in his mind in the post-chaise nearly thirty years before? Could he avoid shaping his past in terms of his present? It is instructive in this respect to compare his narrative with the much more tentative approach of the modern autobiographer Michel Leiris, who has written volume after volume in an attempt to catch his elusive past and present self in words, or with Claude Simon's novel *Histoire*, a first-person narrative where we follow the disordered workings of a man's memory as his present situation impels him to search through his past for clues to understanding his present, but also to avoid those images from the past which cause unbearable pain. Simon's is a rich book, but a record of the failure of a quest. Rousseau's history on the other hand seems to be written without such fundamental misgivings. It is true that he declares himself baffled at times; when he is writing about Madame de Warens he finds it hard to define his feelings intelligibly:

In a word, I was chaste because I loved her. On the basis of these effects, which I have not described well, let anyone who is capable of it say what kind of affection I felt for her. All I can say is that if it already seems very extraordinary, it will seem much more so in what is to come.   (I, 109)

Even here, however, as in the passages where he explains his strange behaviour by reference to contradictory elements in his character, his main problem is to find a way of explaining his feelings in accordance with normal psychology. He does not cast doubt on his memory, and his bafflement has the effect of enhancing the uniqueness of his case.

Rousseau does not therefore deliberately enact for us the difficult search for self-knowledge. He seems to speak with a confident voice, even if he fails to bring his narrative to a satisfactory conclusion or to convince his readers. But his very failure is a strength. Rather than craftily building into his narrative the scepticism which anticipates the reader's objections, he recklessly courts disaster, presenting his critical audience with the image of himself to which he clings. Much of the fascination of the *Confessions* is in following his struggle to create this image, or in the terms used by Huntington Williams, to bring the remembered experiences of his 'actual self' in line with the fundamentally good 'virtual self' constructed in his earlier writings. One needs to remember the remarks from the Neuchâtel preamble to the effect that the autobiographer depicts his present as well as his past. Seen from this perspective, the *Confessions* shows not so much the truth about his earlier life (though this persists as an essential element) as the subsequent forging of a necessary myth, the kind of life-preserving lie about which Nietzsche was to write a century later.

Interpretation

The previous two chapters have shown how the whole work is structured and how the author interprets his life in accordance with his belief in the natural goodness of human beings, and of Jean-Jacques in particular. Philippe Lejeune, a far from unsympathetic reader, describes this as a 'sophism', a logical absurdity forced on Rousseau by his need to feel innocent. In his view, we must read the self-accusation and self-justification of the *Confessions* as unconscious strategies deployed by the author to protect his apparently shameful desires (his masochism for instance) and to display their innocence. By doing so, we can understand and accept a work that would be unacceptable if we tried to take it on the terms offered by the author.

Like many modern readings, this is one which seeks to *interpret* the text. Rousseau does in fact encourage his readers to do this, for instance in the passage at the end of Book 4, where we are asked to reach our own conclusions about the facts presented, or at the beginning of Book 12, where he asks for our collaboration in unravelling the mysteries of the conspiracy. Modern critics, however, tend to interpret the *Confessions* in ways which he would have found unacceptable, bringing to light motivations he sought consciously or unconsciously to repress. The reader (or critic) parts company here with Rousseau's implied reader, who was a partner in an equal exchange. The interpretative critic treats the text as something to be explained, a document which is the product, not only of the author's declared intentions, but of his situation, his desires, his fears, his imagination. From a position outside the text one can hope to understand the author better than he understood himself. And since the *Confessions* offer such a fascinating wealth of information, information which Rousseau hardly seems to have mastered, it is a perfect subject for such critical investigations.

The particular scheme used by Lejeune and other interpreters owes a good deal to the theories of Freud and his followers. Jean Starobinski has written: 'It took Freud to think [i.e. interpret and understand] Rousseau's feelings.' Psychoanalysis is hypothesis rather than truth, of course; in the analysis of literary texts written long ago, it can be considered either as a conjectural approach to the unconscious process which presided over composition, or as a guide for a better reading, which will bring out more fully the complexities that language carries and conceals. The most complete reading of the *Confessions* in this vein is that of J. P. Clément, *Jean-Jacques Rousseau, de l'éros coupable à l'éros glorieux*. This study presents Rousseau's destiny as a story of desire; the author stresses Jean-Jacques's experience of the family, his relations with his father and his search for father and mother substitutes, the importance for him of Aunt Suzanne and of his elder brother, the source of his feelings of guilt and his wish for punishment and failure. His emergence as a successful writer and composer is explained in terms of Freud's theory of sublimation, and the fantasy of the conspiracy, coming after the creative period, is seen as a 'massive return of culpability'. The *Confessions* are a challenge to the unseen enemy who is a projection of the author's feelings of guilt.

Clément's work is influenced by that of Starobinski, not only his book *Jean-Jacques Rousseau, la transparence et l'obstacle*, but also the essay on Rousseau in the first volume of his collection *L'Œil vivant*. Starobinski's aim in these two essential works is a general understanding of Rousseau's life and writings in terms of certain basic impulses, in particular the aspiration to 'transparency' of consciences associated with a lost or imagined paradise. His approach is not strictly Freudian, but is situated at the level of unconscious or semi-conscious drives. In the essay he stresses the role of desire and guilt, connecting them with Jean-Jacques's humiliating experience as a poor child in protestant Geneva, and he interprets his subsequent conduct and books as a compensatory strategy, in which he strives to regain his innocence in the world of the imagination and to interpret his life on the model of the great religious myths of his childhood – Paradise, Fall, Exile, Martyrdom. This attempt to overcome life's contradictions could not ultimately succeed; Rousseau is, however, an exemplary modern writer in that he concludes the 'dangerous pact of the self with language', accepting not just to write about himself and his problems, but to embody them in the very manner of his writing. Starobinski's work is in my view the most impressive attempt at a global explanation of Rousseau's career and of the signification of the *Confessions* in it. It avoids the reductive approach of those medical interpretations which do not so much explain as explain away, suggesting that we need not take seriously the words of a man whose interesting case can be labelled with the terms of a psychiatric textbook (this is one of the dangers of the author's own insistence on his uniqueness). In Starobinski's studies, even if a note of censure can be heard, Rousseau is seen as a remarkable human being seeking in his writing to come to terms with existence.

There are numerous other modern accounts of Rousseau's life, works and career, which take the *Confessions* as an essential document, if not as the principal object of study. The two major biographies of J. Guehenno and L. G. Crocker constantly confront the autobiography with other sources and show how Rousseau arranges his memories in the interests of a certain view of himself. Guehenno does so with the sympathy of a friend, Crocker in the more superior manner of one who knows enough to pity or condemn the man, while admitting the vast importance of his work. In rather different ways, R. Grimsley's *Rousseau, a Study in Self-Awareness* and H. Williams's *Rousseau and Romantic Autobiography* treat the autobiographical writings as attempts to create a unified self-image with which to confront an unsatisfactory world. Grimsley's main stress is on the problems of Rousseau the man, and he says little of the *Confessions* except as a document, whereas Williams, following in the line of Jacques Derrida (*De la grammatologie*) and Paul de Man (*Allegories of Reading*), concentrates more on the books themselves and the author's creation of a 'textual world'.

A different and very interesting approach might be derived from that of Michel Launay in his *Jean-Jacques Rousseau, écrivain politique*. This book does not specifically concern the autobiography, but shows in detail the importance of Jean-Jacques's early social experiences, his *déclassement* and his first-hand experience of the struggles of Geneva for an understanding of his political ideas. The *Confessions* are the history of his inner life, it is true, but this inner life is largely shaped by social experience. The work does not simply describe his acquaintance with servitude and freedom, it is a reaction to it, an attempt to place its author in relation to this complex and uncomfortable world. It is important therefore, as we read his description of his Genevan childhood or of Madame d'Epinay's circle, to bear in mind that this is the work of the Genevan apprentice who has lived in France, a poor man among the rich, a commoner among the titled.

These are some of the ways in which modern criticism has sought to come to terms with the *Confessions* by trying to unearth their author's fundamental project in writing, and I have drawn on them in the earlier chapters of this study. In some cases the explanations, while being given from the perspective of an outsider, do not differ widely from Rousseau's own perceptions, in others he would certainly have rejected the explanations offered. There is some discomfort here for the interpreter, since he or she may come to sound superior to a writer who is after all vastly more important than any of those who claim to understand him better than he understood himself. Perhaps this is inseparable from the activity of literary criticism; the critic comes after the event, and if critical understanding is to be more than repetition or resurrection, he or she must go beyond the author's own understanding of the work. In the same way as Rousseau himself set out to understand inequality by devising the explanatory model of natural man, so the critic seeks to construct a model (of Rousseau, his writings, his situation) in order to understand the *Confessions*. The danger is that in thinking to improve on the author's own deluded self-awareness, the critic too may fall into the trap for biographers and make up 'ingenious novels built on . . . subtle conjectures where the author is more intent on being brilliant than on finding the truth' (I, 1149).

Autobiography and fiction

If only by taking into account Rousseau's other writings, all the readings I have mentioned, including my own, have taken seriously the autobiographical status of the *Confessions*, seeking to see them in their often oblique relation to a real man and his problems. This seems the obvious thing to do. But how in fact can one distinguish between an autobiography and a first-person novel which can be read as a free-standing work of art, without reference to the person who signed it? We have seen how Rousseau shapes his life, creating himself as one might create a character in a novel. In the subtlety with which he is drawn, Jean-Jacques is far and away more interesting than the heroes of most novels. Should we not go one stage further and say, as Roland Barthes wrote at the outset of his own 'autobiography': 'All this must be considered as spoken by a character in a novel'?

This might seem an ideal solution to the problems raised so far in this chapter. We should no longer need to concern ourselves with the truth to any one man's experience of the life-story we are reading. No one complains that Defoe in his life of Robinson Crusoe does not stick faithfully to the story of Alexander Selkirk. Novelists are free, constrained only by the bounds of plausibility within which convention requires them to work. In the case of the *Confessions*, however, this perspective will yield something very different from the *Robinson Crusoe* type of memoir novel. The hero is not only the young Jean-Jacques, making his picaresque then tragic way through the world, it is equally the ageing narrator, struggling to create a satisfactory image of himself against a hostile society. It does not matter then if he is what modern criticism might call an 'unreliable narrator'; so much the better, one might say, provided he offers a telling representation of human problems and passions.

In this respect it is enlightening to set the *Confessions* alongside a work written a hundred years later, Dostoevsky's *Notes from Underground*. This short book is a self-portrait, including a good deal of past-tense narrative. The narrator – who is far from believing in natural goodness – presents himself in his relations with others – in contradictory relations of excessive affection and prickly hostility. It is very like Rousseau at times, though much blacker and more twisted, and even includes a scene parallel to that in Book 9 where Grimm and Madame d'Epinay sit down to supper while the excluded Jean-Jacques walks up and down fuming with resentment. As we read the *Notes*, however, we know we are reading the words of a fictitious character. The challenges issued by the narrator to his reader must be distinguished from the communication between author and real reader; the author speaks to us (not without irony) in editorial notes.

However much we may speculate about the relation between Dostoevsky and his hero, the text is not autobiographical. Almost certainly, as in most worthwhile novels, the reader will feel deeply involved with the fictional hero, but always with the distancing awareness that he is a verbal construct. Our judgement on him is not a judgement on a real person. No one is trying to address us directly.

Cannot the narrator and the hero of the *Confessions* also be regarded as fictional beings, as if Jean-Jacques Rousseau had never existed, and the whole thing had been made up by some anonymous author for our interest, edification and pleasure? From early on, this is how the work was regarded by one or two readers − such at least seems to be the implication of Friedrich Schlegel's remark of 1800: 'In my view, Rousseau's *Confessions* is a remarkable novel; his *Nouvelle Héloïse* is only mediocre.' Most early readers did not see it this way at all, being interested exclusively in the documentary aspect of the work. Gradually, however, the aesthetic approach came to the fore. Critics began to write of the charm of certain episodes (usually in Part I), of the role of imagination, the eloquence, the psychological penetration, the artistic structure, the narrative skill. It is significant that in a work entitled *Rousseau et l'art du roman* J. L. Lecercle devotes almost as much space to the *Confessions* as to *La Nouvelle Héloïse*.

For Rousseau himself it would have been absolutely per-verse to read his autobiography as one might read a novel. He was well aware of the danger that readers may transform any written work into a work of art, the better to ignore the author's message. Not long before beginning the *Confessions* he wrote in the preface to the *Letters from the Mountain*: 'I beg my readers to ignore my beautiful style and simply to examine whether my reasons are good or bad.' As for the autobiographical writings, he describes the way in which a fellow-writer (Condillac) commented on his *Dialogues*:

He spoke to me of this work as he would have spoken of a literary work which I had asked him to read and give me his opinion on. He spoke of rearrangements I could make so as to present my material in a better order; but he said nothing to me of the effect my writing had had on him or what he thought of the author.   (I, 982)

The suggestion is that an aesthetic reading is one that avoids responsibility, failing to answer the writer's perilous commitment in kind. In the same way it has been suggested that to concentrate on the charm and imaginative power of Rousseau's writing may be a way of deflecting attention from the uncomfortable challenges he poses to our society and its culture.

Of course nothing obliges us to accept or observe what Philippe Lejeune calls the 'autobiographical pact', to read the *Confessions* on the assumption that Rousseau the character and narrator and Rousseau the author and historical personage share the same identity, and that this commits us to a particular mode of reading. On the other hand, however much aesthetic pleasure one may gain from the book, one would miss a great deal if one read it essentially as a work of the imagination. One of the peculiar interests of autobiography is precisely the tension between what Aristotle called history and poetry − how things happened and how they might have happened. The *Confessions* are both document and monument; the author is a creator, but also a man exposing himself dangerously (like the matador to the horn of the bull, as Michel Leiris puts it in his *L'Age d'homme*). One may not always believe Rousseau's account of his life and thoughts, but one should believe at least that it is an attempt to tell the truth and not a work of fantasy. The *Confessions* show the difficult negotiation between the world of 'beings after my own heart' and the experiences that life actually brought to the writer. I do not believe therefore that one should seek to evade the discomforts engendered by Rousseau's endeavours to convince his reader. One does well to put oneself in the position of the earlier audiences, challenged to judge, rather than in that of Condillac, content to appreciate. If we do so, we shall be impelled − and this is the great virtue of the *Confessions* − to consider our own lives, how truthfully we know and tell them, how they can be justified.

For or against?

The judgements that Rousseau presses on us are not only concerned with truth-telling and sincerity. One is asked also to say if the Jean-Jacques one comes to know is a *good* man, or at least if he is a man one can take to one's heart. On such issues he is uncompromising. One example is the long auto-biographical letter he wrote to Hume in July 1766. Presenting the 'facts of the case' in accordance with his view of things, and with considerable forensic skill, he offers Hume a choice: 'If he [Hume] was not the best of men, he would have to be the most evil' (*Corr.* XXX, 35). Naturally this implies a judgement on himself too; if Hume is good, Rousseau is wickedly ungrateful, but if Hume is a false friend, Rousseau is vindicated. It is all or nothing, friend or foe. 'To be loved by all who came near me was always my keenest desire'; the reader is asked to join the loving circle, to enter the author's world, to accept the demanding conditions he imposed on his friends. And because such a demand is felt to be excessive and embarrassing, the reader may well choose the part of enemy instead. Rousseau has retained his power to divide readers. And when I say 'Rousseau', I mean not just the author of the books — though there have been violent reactions to such works as the *Social Contract* — but the man, or what we take to be the man. With a novelist like Balzac or a poet like Keats it is probably immaterial whether the reader feels affection for the author who is lost behind (or within) the texts. Rousseau on the other hand, by putting himself immodestly to the fore, presses us to respond to him as a person.

He was a saint for many of his early readers, a devil for others. The violence with which critics have continued to attack him — as a person — is extraordinary, and the *Confessions* have provided a good deal of their ammunition. The main heads of the accusation have usually been that he is self-obsessed, vain, self-righteous, hypocritical, ungrateful, disloyal, vindictive, mean — and none of these are entirely without foundation. It needs to be said, however, that this hostility, particularly in the early days, was often snobbish.

Sometimes this appears openly in criticisms of the *Confessions*; on the publication of Part I, Madame de Boufflers, his former friend and protector, likened it to 'the work of a farm-hand, or someone even lower'. For such critics, Rousseau is a base-born person, eaten up with resentment, and compensating for his humiliation with the monstrous pride of the *parvenu*. He lacks the inborn tact of those who know that it is unbecoming to speak too much about yourself, and that hyperbole is a sign of bad taste. Conversely the biographer Jean Guehenno has written, with some exaggeration: 'All those who come from the common people can find an echo of themselves in him.'

The social shades into the political. Rousseau was highly honoured by the Revolution, and his admirer Ginguené wrote in 1791 that he 'was only persecuted by despotism because he called men back to [their] ancient freedom'. It was Rousseau and not Voltaire and the Encyclopedists, who was adopted as a patron saint by Robespierre and the more radical French revolutionaries. When one knows about subsequent French (or indeed British) attitudes to Robespierre, it is not surprising that Rousseau has been the target for a good deal of abuse over the last two hundred years. As Raymond Trousson wrote recently, in a discussion of reactions to the work in the nineteenth century, 'until 1912 judgements on the *Confessions* are almost invariably inseparable from certain [political] commitments'.

This political explanation is helpful, but not sufficient. By no means all the critics of the *Confessions* have been reactionary members of the privileged classes. Nor have all its admirers been radicals and plebeians. Those who love Rousseau do so for many reasons. And just as his critics will almost always admit the value of much of his writing, so his apologists, with a few exceptions, have not felt able to admire him as he would have wished. On the strength of the *Confessions*, let alone the other documents we possess, it is hard to believe that he was as good a man as any who ever lived, that he was utterly free of hate, envy and malice, and that all his actions sprang from innocent motives. Almost all readers must feel inclined from time to time to laugh at what they take to be Rousseau's self-deception, and one may well suspect that in practice it would have been hard to avoid the exasperated reactions of Diderot or Madame d'Epinay. One may also feel that Rousseau, like many of his contemporaries, makes unfortunate assumptions about women, whose role in providing a much-needed support system is taken for granted, while public life, authorship and a certain kind of friendship are reserved for men. Feminist criticism of Rousseau has concentrated more on the advocacy of male dominance in *Emile* and the *Letter to d'Alembert*, but the autobiography too, with its images of woman as mother, provider and tempter, reflects a view of male–female relationships which may make the modern reader uneasy. Whether as actor or as narrator, the Rousseau of the *Confessions* is not always an easy person to love. Even so, in spite of his all-or-nothing statements, I do not think such reservations need prevent us from entering Rousseau's world, not as disciples or hero-worshippers, but as fellow human beings, or even as friends. This may sound simple-minded. How can one regard as a friend a man who died more than two hundred years ago and whose only tangible trace is a collection of written words which we now interpret as we think fit? Is it not better to forget his deluded appeal for a personal link with the reader and content oneself with reaction to the books as books? Perhaps, yet the exceptional thing about Rousseau is precisely his insane ambition to make his speaking voice reach us across (or through) his written pages. And it works. There are few authors, I think, whose writing succeeds so fully, for better or worse, in making them present to the reader.

If one can react to Rousseau with this kind of fellow-feeling, this must mean that he is not so totally unlike every-one else as the opening page of the *Confessions* announces. The contradiction between his claim to be exceptional and his desire to provide a useful 'point of comparison' is more apparent than real. Jean-Jacques is unique, but so is everyone. Although we may feel that there is something regressive and infantile in his image of paradise, there is still a powerful appeal in this ageing man's evocation of childhood and youth, and above all in his poetry of ordinary existence. Sinking a well deep into his past, he sets free springs of life that all people can share, and that had been largely ignored by most literature before him. He writes of desires that may take strange forms, but that are widely shared, the need for love and a loving community, the love of liberty and impatience with servitude, the desire to be oneself and to find one's own happiness. These carried him into all kinds of inextricable and tragic contradictions, peculiar to him, no doubt, but having their equivalent in the lives of many people. In his *Confessions* he plunges us deep into this turmoil, with self-deception, but also with an intensity that makes him, to quote Guehenno again, 'an extraordinary résumé of the modern human condition'. Like many of the great modern writers, he is exasperating, he is mad if you like, but much of his power is in his madness, his ability to embarrass and provoke. One could say of him what a modern reader has said of Victor Hugo: 'What I like in him, is his willingness to put his foot in it.' I should not have written this book if I did not think of the author of the *Confessions* with affection and admiration.

Conclusion: the place of the 'Confessions'

After writing about the problems posed by the *Confessions* for the reader (including myself), it remains for me to say a word in more objective terms about the place of the work in French and European literature. Whether one likes it or not, Rousseau's autobiography is one of the key texts of modern literature, breaking new ground in a quite exceptional way.

We need not be greatly concerned here with the wave of Rousseauism that affected most countries in Europe in the second half of the eighteenth century. The *Confessions* played their part in this, in that they helped to fix the hero's image, but they were published long after the works which had established Rousseau's reputation, in particular *Emile* and *La Nouvelle Héloïse*. What is more, although they were the subject of intense curiosity, they met with a generally reserved or hostile reception in France, even among the author's admirers – there were, of course, notable exceptions, such as Ginguené, whose admiring *Letters on the Confessions of Jean-Jacques Rousseau* (1791) bring out the usefulness, beauty and human appeal of the work with great perspicacity. In Britain too the dominant reaction, in the press at least, was unfavourable; this was soon reinforced by Burke's description of Rousseau as the 'philosopher of vanity'. It seems in fact that in the early years the *Confessions* were fully appreciated above all by German readers; writers such as Goethe, Schiller, Wieland, F. Schlegel and E. T. A. Hoffmann spoke of them with great enthusiasm. But everywhere, in spite of the hostile judgements of many critics, the great interest of the biographical material guaranteed that the work would continue to attract readers, if only for the shocking passages. There have been numerous editions and translations into many languages, and it has doubtless been read by millions of people in the two centuries following its publication. A number of famous anthology passages, mainly taken from Part I, have contributed to the stock of romantic imagery (lakes, mountains, walking, dreaming) which is often associated with their author's name. It is however mainly in the last fifty years or so that the *Confessions* have come to be appreciated as a work of art in their own right, a monument rather than a document, and indeed the pinnacle of Rousseau's achievement.

'Poor Rousseau', said Carlyle, 'a morbid, excitable, spasmodic man, a fanatic, a sadly contracted hero' – but in everything he touched on, this poor madman opened new ways to those who came after him, in the novel, in political philosophy, in education, and for modern times most of all in autobiography. The *Confessions* (together with the *Reveries*) can fairly be seen as the fountain head of modern writing about the self. As we saw in chapter 2, there were great precursors, above all Montaigne. There were accounts of the spiritual itineraries of pietists or quietists, not meant usually for public consumption. And there were the innumerable memoirs of public figures, who might on occasion lift a corner of the curtain surrounding their private lives. What Rousseau did was to bring these streams together and virtually create the modern literary genre of autobiography.

The *Confessions* are not memoirs, in which the interest lies primarily in people, events or milieus to which the author bears witness. They tell rather of the inner development of an individual, the formation of a personality. The individual in question is not a statesman, general or courtier, but a commoner. It is true that he is a famous writer – indeed one can see the *Confessions* as the beginning of that characteristic modern genre, the autobiography of the man of letters. But Jean-Jacques does not become a writer or a famous man until Book 8; for most of the work he is an ordinary person, even if the author regards his personality as unique. The reader is invited to give to the thoughts and feelings of this obscure individual the attention normally (until then) reserved for the more exalted figures of tragedy and history.

One should not exaggerate Rousseau's originality in this respect. The decades before he wrote had seen the appearance of the serious novel of ordinary life, as exemplified in the work of Richardson, Marivaux and Prévost — or indeed his own *La Nouvelle Héloïse*. The *Confessions* owe a good deal to this tradition, just as they contribute to the enormous development of the realist novel in the nineteenth century. Stendhal's *The Scarlet and the Black*, for instance, can be seen as echoing Rousseau's autobiography, as can all the novels of education (*Bildungsromane*) which pay particular attention to the formative years of the hero. For it is in the representation of childhood above all that he is a pioneer. He knew, like Wordsworth, that 'the child is father to the man'. One of the unsolved questions in literary history is that of Wordsworth's debt to Rousseau; we know that he possessed the *Confessions*, but there is nothing to show whether this influenced the writing of the *Prelude*. Be that as it may, the two works together establish childhood as a central concern of literature. William Hazlitt, a great admirer of both writers, saw in Rousseau the originator of that poetry of childhood which has been so important in Romantic and post-Romantic writing, and which only appears in the most fleeting way in the writing of earlier periods. The poetry of memory too, and we have had occasion to note how in this respect the *Confessions* anticipate the work of a very different writer, Marcel Proust. In all this, Rousseau set flowing springs which seem to have become increasingly necessary to the modern world.

More generally, Rousseau's example did a great deal to impose the apparently trivial details which so shocked early readers as worthy of interest, indeed as occupying a vital place in the life of the individual. The picture of the popes in the study at Bossey has had an immense progeny in all the autobiographies, journals and other kinds of personal writing which have appeared in such numbers over the last two hundred years. So too has the spanking at Bossey. Stendhal, whose *Life of Henry Brulard* is one of the great autobiographies of the nineteenth century, wrote with gratitude that 'the empire of the ridiculous has shrunk today, and that is the work of Jean-Jacques Rousseau'. Rousseau's frankness, whatever its psychological origins, opens the doors on dark areas of life which most previous (and many subsequent) writers preferred to shroud in dignified silence. The *Confessions*, in fact, illuminate not so much the public life as all that is private and secret. No doubt Plutarch and Montaigne were powerful aids to Rousseau as he explored this treacherous *terra incognita*, but even more than they – and in spite of his self-deception and myth-making – he presses on his readers the absorbing interest of the self, his individual self, the self that manifests itself so unmistakeably in the writing. This concentration on the self (so different from the unreflecting 'love of self' of Rousseau's natural man) has been regarded by many as morbid and dangerous, the sign of a sick society, the source of all kinds of miseries. Conversely it has been seen as the proper recognition of the value of the individual personality, considered no longer in relation to God, but as the supreme source of value in human life. In any case, for better or worse, the period between about 1750 and 1800 is marked in Western European literature by an extraordinary shift of emphasis from the work of art as aesthetic creation to the work of art as expression of the writer's inner being. In this movement the *Confessions* are an essential text.

Guide to further reading

I. Works by Rousseau

The most important of Rousseau's works are mentioned in chapters 1 and 2. The standard French edition of the works is that published in the Bibliothèque de la Pléiade (Gallimard) under the general editorship of Marcel Raymond and Bernard Gagnebin (4 vols. to date, Paris, 1959–69); the autobiographical writings are in volume I. There is an excellent edition of the *Confessions* by J. Voisine in the Classiques Garnier (Paris, 1964). Over the last two hundred years there have been many different English-language editions of the *Confessions*, not a few of them abridged or bowdlerised. Of the two most readily available complete versions the first, a reissue of an older translation, was published in Dent's Everyman Library in 1931; it is at present out of print, but there is a considerably shortened version of the same text edited by L. G. Crocker in the American Pocket Books series. The other is a generally more lively and up-to-date translation by J. M. Cohen, first published in the Penguin Classics in 1953; this appears to be the only complete English version currently in print. A less accessible but very handsome publication is the limited edition produced by the Nonesuch Press in 1938, a revision of the original English translations (1783–90). See also the *Reveries of the Solitary Walker*, translated by P. France (Penguin Books, 1979).

II. Critical studies

Comments on important contributions will be found in chapter 5. For a reading of the *Confessions* some of the most useful studies in English are:

J. H. Broome, *Rousseau, a Study of his Thought* (London, 1963)

L. G. Crocker, *Jean-Jacques Rousseau* (2 vols., New York, 1968–73)

M. B. Ellis, *Rousseau's Venetian Story* (Baltimore, 1966)

R. J. Ellrich, *Rousseau and his Reader* (Chapel Hill, 1969)

R. Grimsley, *Jean-Jacques Rousseau, a Study in Self-Awareness* (Cardiff, 1969)

J. Guehenno, *Jean-Jacques Rousseau* translated by J. and D. Weightman (2 vols., London 1966)

H. Williams, *Rousseau and Romantic Autobiography* (Oxford, 1983).

There is a vast literature in French. The books which I have found most helpful for understanding various aspects of Rousseau's autobiography are:

P.-P. Clément, *Jean-Jacques Rousseau, de l'éros coupable à l'éros glorieux* (Neuchâtel, 1976)

J. Derrida, *De la grammatologie* (Paris 1967)

M. Launay, *Jean-Jacques Rousseau, écrivain politique (1712–1762)* (Grenoble, 1971)

J.-L. Lecercle, *Rousseau et l'art du roman* (Paris, 1962)

P. Lejeune, *Le Pacte autobiographique* (Paris, 1975)

M. Raymond, *Jean-Jacques Rousseau; la quête de soi et la rêverie* (Paris, 1962)

H. de Saussure, *Rousseau et les manuscrits des Confessions* (Paris, 1958)

J. Starobinski, *Jean-Jacques Rousseau, la transparence et l'obstacle* (2nd edition, Paris, 1971)
  L'Œil vivant (Paris, 1961)
  La Relation critique (Paris, 1970)

J. Voisine, *Jean-Jacques Rousseau en Angleterre à l'époque romantique* (Paris, 1956).

There are useful articles in a great many publications, including the *Annales de la Société Jean-Jacques Rousseau* (Geneva, 1905– , 37 vols. to date), and *Jean-Jacques Rousseau et son œuvre* (Paris, 1964). For the reception of the *Confessions* see the special number of the journal *Œuvres et critiques*, III, i (1978). A recent brief student guide in French is that by J. Dubosclard in the Hatier 'Profil d'une œuvre' series (Paris, 1984).

III. Autobiography

After many years of neglect, a lot has been written on this subject recently, particularly in the USA. The following contain interesting discussions:

R. Pascal, *Design and Truth in Autobiography* (Cambridge, Mass., 1960)

J. Olney (ed.), *Autobiography* (Princeton, 1980)

P. Lejeune, *L'Autobiographie en France* (Paris, 1971)
  Le Pacte autobiographique (Paris, 1975)

Revue de l'histoire littéraire de France, 1975, no. 6 (special number on autobiography).

It is well worth comparing the *Confessions* with other classics of the genre such as St Augustine's *Confessions*, Montaigne's *Essays*, Wordsworth's *Prelude*, Goethe's *Dichtung und Wahrheit* and Stendhal's *Life of Henry Brulard*, as well as with some of the innumerable modern attempts at autobiography.